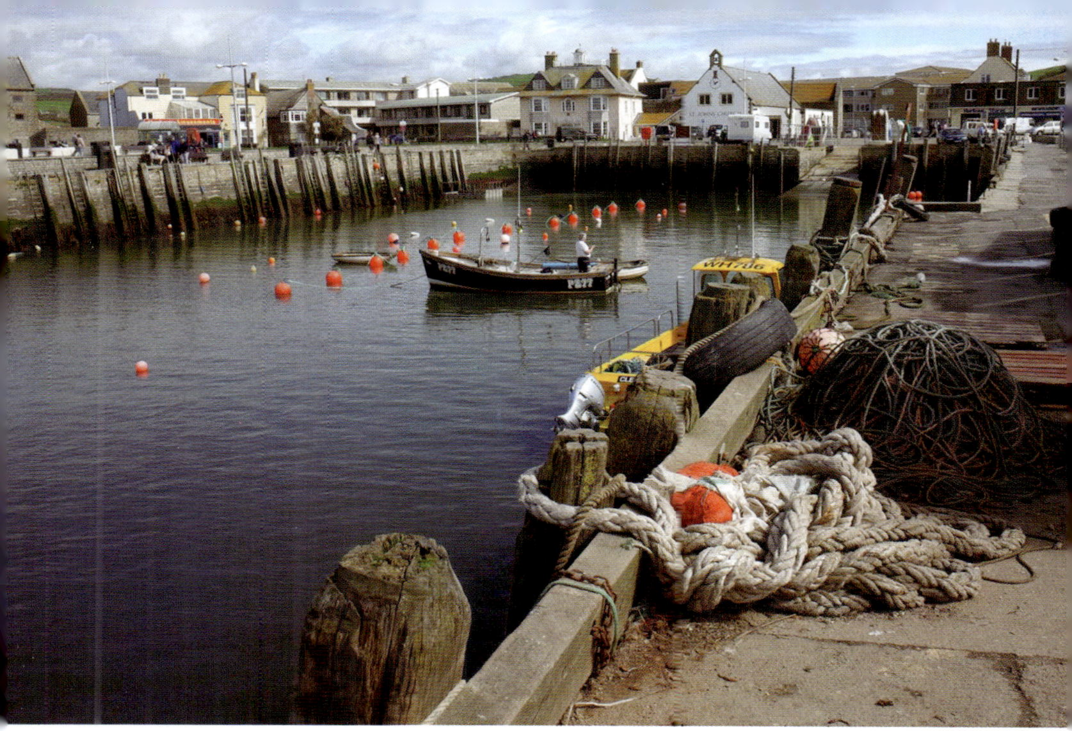

# *More Dorset* SMUGGLERS' PUBS

**Terry Townsend**

**To my wife Carol**
with thanks for her continued
patience, help and support

First published in Great Britain in 2019

Copyright © Terry Townsend 2019

All rights reserved. No part of this publication may be reproduced, stored in a retrieval system, or transmitted in any form or by any means without the prior permission of the copyright holder.

British Library Cataloguing-in-Publication Data
A CIP record for this title is available from the British Library

ISBN 978 0 85710 117 4

**PiXZ Books**
Halsgrove House, Ryelands Business Park,
Bagley Road, Wellington, Somerset TA21 9PZ
Tel: 01823 653777
Fax: 01823 216796
email: sales@halsgrove.com

An imprint of Halstar Ltd, part of the Halsgrove group of companies
Information on all Halsgrove titles is available at: www.halsgrove.com

Printed and bound in India by
Parksons Graphics

# Prologue

When researching and writing *Dorset Smugglers' Pubs* it soon became apparent I had a problem. My criteria for selecting the featured pubs was a strong smuggling connection combined with a welcoming experience for present day visitors. However, there was simply too much interesting and relevant information – not to mention great photographic opportunities. In the end I was obliged to overlook a number of special pubs and inns whose stories deserved to be told.

In the first book I explained how smuggling in the county began in the eighteenth century and developed into a way of life lasting the best part of a hundred and fifty years. This means every Dorset hostelry of sufficient antiquity has its share of smugglers' tales. Luckily the initial book was very well received which has enabled me to proceed with this second volume.

Once again I travelled to towns, villages and hamlets across Dorset seeking the former meeting places of the fearless men who called themselves 'free traders'. Most people who enjoy visiting old pubs and inns do so because they feel a vague sense of history but I believe the pleasure can be greatly enhanced if the real facts are known.

*Terry Townsend*
*Dorset, 2019*

The romantic image of the pirate-like smuggler is more folklore than fact.

## ACKNOWLEDGEMENTS

Thanks once again to the old team for their encouragement and practical help – Adrienne Bradney-Smith and Brenda and Tony Stables.

Plus a special thank you to Karen Binaccioni for her expert contribution with layout and design.

**TERRY TOWNSEND'S OTHER HALSGROVE TITLES INCLUDE:**
*Once Upon a Pint – A Readers' Guide to the Literary Pubs & Inns of Dorset & Somerset*

*Dorset Smugglers' Pubs,*
*East Cornwall Smugglers' Pubs: Kingsand to Mevagissey*
*East Devon Smugglers' Pubs*
*Hampshire Smugglers' Pubs*
*Isle of Wight Smugglers' Pubs*
*Kent Smugglers' Pubs*
*Suffolk Smugglers' Pubs*
*West Cornwall Smugglers' Pubs: St Ives to Falmouth*

*Bristol & Clifton Slave Trade Trails*

*Jane Austen & Bath*
*Jane Austen's Hampshire*
*Jane Austen's Kent*

# CONTENTS

**Introduction**: *An Everyday Story of Country Folk* ................8

### THE PUBS

1  Abbotsbury, *The Ilchester Arms* ................23
2  Bere Regis, *The Drax Arms* ................29
3  Burton Bradstock, *Three Horseshoes* ................34
4  Cerne Abbas, *The Royal Oak* ................41
5  Chaldon Herring, *Sailor's Return* ................48
6  Chideock, *George Inn* ................55
7  Corfe Castle, *The Greyhound Inn* ................62
8  Corscombe, *The Fox Inn* ................71
9  Farnham, *The Museum* ................77
10  Fiddleford, *Fiddleford Inn* ................83
11  Kingston, *Scott Arms* ................91
12  Piddletrenthide, *Piddle Inn* ................97
13  Puncknowle, *Crown Inn* ................103
14  Symondsbury, *Ilchester Arms* ................108
15  West Bay, *Bridport Arms* ................113
16  Wimborne, *The Olive Branch* ................121

**Selected Bibliography** ................128

**KEY TO MAP**
(1) Abbotsbury, The Ilchester Arms
(2) Bere Regis, The Drax Arms
(3) Burton Bradstock, Three Horseshoes
(4) Cerne Abbas, The Royal Oak
(5) Chaldon Herring, Sailor's Return
(6) Chideock, George Inn
(7) Corfe Castle, The Greyhound Inn
(8) Corscombe, The Fox Inn
(9) Farnham, The Museum

(10) Fiddleford, Fiddleford Inn
(11) Kingston, Scott Arms
(12) Piddletrenthide, Piddle Inn
(13) Puncknowle, Crown Inn
(14) Symondsbury, Ilchester Arms
(15) West Bay, Bridport Arms
(16) Wimborne, The Olive Branch

# Introduction

## An Everyday Story of Country Folk

From around 1700 Britain was waging war in some part of the world well-nigh continuously against the forces of France, Holland, Spain and eventually the American colonists. By the mid eighteenth century foreign war had become an accepted way of life in these islands.

To fund the conflicts, successive governments imposed taxes on the importation of a wide range of luxury goods such as brandy, tobacco, tea and fine silks. Thus the law makers unwittingly created a climate for the establishment of serious organised crime.

The taxes were unpopular with most of society and widely resented by a rural population often close to starvation. However, this black cloud came with the opportunity of a silver lining. Buying tax-free goods abroad and selling to an eager home market was a very profitable, if somewhat dangerous pastime. This 'free trading' as it became known to those involved, was an inevitable result of punitive taxation.

In Dorset a significant cross section of the population supplemented their meagre incomes by smuggling. Most of them were poor farm labourers.

The illegal practice grew to enormous proportions becoming an important element of the country's economy. All classes of society became involved and support for smuggling extended to churchmen, magistrates and the aristocracy. The squire, the parson and the clerk frequently connived in smuggling operations; buying contraband, financing smuggling runs and protecting smugglers from the law.

Smugglers subsequently have often been romanticised as cheeky rogues. The Victorians had a fascination for smugglers and fanciful illustrations of the time have helped create a general misconception. Even today many people entertain an image of a smuggler as a Cornish mariner dressed like a pirate and carrying a cask of spirits on his shoulder – a veritable sea-booted Robin Hood delivering some of life's little luxuries at affordable prices to the rural poor.

In reality, the unlawful practice of running contraband was conducted in all coastal counties of Southern and Eastern England. Dorset, with its large tracts of isolated countryside adjoining the coast, was ideally suited to these activities. Goods landed in coves and on open beaches were distributed throughout the country, very often by people who had never seen the sea. The phrase: *'carried off by the country people'* appears regularly in Customs Reports of the period when referencing failed seizure of goods.

A significant cross section of Dorset folk supplemented their meagre incomes by moonlighting on *moonless* nights! Butchers, bakers and candlestick makers turned their hands to smuggling when the opportunity presented itself. Such people as these were part of the army of land smugglers who vastly outnumbered their seagoing contemporaries.

One man in particular emerging from these ranks in a rag to riches story is Isaac Gulliver who spent a large part of his career in East Dorset and is featured in detail in the concluding chapter of this book. Gulliver died in his house in Wimborne and was buried with some ceremony in the town's minster church.

Isaac Gulliver, who emerged as 'King of Dorset smugglers'.

A sample of less fortunate Dorset smugglers tried at Lyme Regis assizes shows how whole communities were involved. Listed occupations included quarryman, tin-plate worker, ferryman, cooper, flax dresser, innkeeper, bricklayer, pig jobber, miller, shoemaker and fell-monger (hide dealer) although the majority of apprehended villains were simple farm labourers.

It was not just men who were deeply involved. The register of inmates serving time in Dorchester Gaol between 1782 and 1853 records names and occupations of no fewer than 64 women convicted of various smuggling related offences including lighting cliff-top warning fires and hiding and distributing illegal goods.

The records contain the names of women like Maria Bagwell, dressmaker; Ann Gummer, needlewoman; Martha Lumb, charwoman; Martha Vivian, labourer; Levia Rutledge and Mercy Way, twine spinners and Catherine Winter, a Weymouth seamstress who served an eighteen-day sentence in 1844 for smuggling at the age of seventy!

The greatest authority on this aspect of Dorset life was novelist and poet Thomas Hardy. His birthplace cottage at Higher Bockhampton lay on the free trader's route between Osmington Mills and eager customers in Sherborne, Yeovil and manor houses along the way. The Bockhampton cottage was actually a capacious safe house for smuggled contraband

Thomas Hardy's birthplace at Higher Bockhampton was a capacious safe house for smuggled brandy accommodating up to 80 casks at a time.

accommodating up to eighty 4½ gallon casks of brandy known as 'half ankers'.

As a child, Hardy was regaled with smuggling stories from his grandfather and his father's manservant. The health of this old retainer had been ruined by his working as a nocturnal 'tub carrier'; stumbling miles over steep and rough terrain hauling the crushing weight of 4½ gallon casks, two and even three at a time, slung with a rope harness on his back and chest.

## The Distracted Preacher

As a child, Thomas Hardy was regaled with true-life Dorset smuggling stories from his grandfather and an old family retainer.

Hardy used his intimate knowledge of Dorset smuggling practices as background for his (long) short story *The Distracted Preacher* from his collection of *Wessex Tales*. Presented as a romance the narrative is also an accurate guide to the refinement of methods used during smuggling's heyday.

The story concerns young Wesleyan preacher Robert Stockdale temporarily seconded to pastoral duties in the village of Nether-Moynton (the real life Owermoigne). He secures lodgings in the house of youthful widow Lizzie Newberry who lives with and supports her elderly, infirm mother.

Robert and Lizzie are soon attracted to each other but an insurmountable obstacle to the fulfilment of their love soon reveals itself. Lizzie, in partnership with her cousin local miller Jim Owlett, has taken over the role from her departed husband as one of the chief organisers of the local smuggling enterprise. Stockdale believes in the teachings of John Wesley who declared smuggling to be an accursed thing. As a law-abiding citizen, he also feels a loyalty to the king.

INTRODUCTION

The minister first arriving in Nether-Moynton is suffering from a bad cold. Although his domain is the Methodist chapel he discovers on the first evening contraband spirits are hidden in the church and that Lizzie not only has access to the tubs, which she explains are called 'things' by the villagers, but knows exactly how secretly to broach one, leaving no trace of disturbance, so he can take a drop of medicinal brandy.

Eventually Stockdale realises that everyone in the village, including the members of his congregation, are involved in smuggling and that the enterprise is highly organised. Being concerned about Lizzie's safety he follows her during one of her night-time excursions along an established smugglers route known and described by Hardy.

Hardy's father's manservant had ruined his health by frequently hauling the crushing weight of 9 to 12 gallons of brandy for miles over steep, rough terrain.

The minister takes a lane from the village which leads immediately across the present A352 and heads off over Gallows Hill to the tiny hamlet of Holworth; a sizeable village at the

In addition to Owermoigne, churches and churchyard tombs across Dorset were regularly used for concealing contraband.

13

This typical Victorian aquatint shows a smuggler loading a pistol while another hurriedly hides a tub of spirits in the cellar.

time but now consisting of two farms and a pillar-box. Beyond Holworth a chalk track leads directly over the magnificent empty downs to the Ringworth Shore (Ringstead Bay) with its mile of golden curving beach backed by tumbled grassy hills rising to five hundred feet. Lizzie Newberry – and the real life smugglers – took this route on their nocturnal expeditions.

The landing is aborted because Preventive Men are present in the area and Stockdale observes Lizzie lighting a warning fire. On the following night, after crossing the main road, Lizzie turns east along the hillside and then south over Lord's Barrow to Chaldon with its old smugglers' pub *The Sailor's Return*. From Chaldon she proceeds to Daggers Grave (Daggers Gate) on her way to the arranged landing site at Lulwind (Lulworth Cove) where, from the cliff's edge, the smugglers descended by rope to the beach.

The contraband landing site of Ringworth Shore (Ringstead Bay) with its mile of golden curving beach backed by tumbled grassy hills rising to 500 feet.

On questioning Lizzie, Stockdale learns that smuggling is a winter pursuit undertaken in the early hours of a 'dark', the name given to the period 'between the moons' when barrels of contraband spirits are unloaded at nearby locations along the coast. Three alternative drop points are arranged for each run, providing an opportunity to evade patrolling Preventive Men. If there is any danger of being discovered, ships are warned off by lighting a beacon on the headlands. If all three attempts are abandoned the casks are weighted, strung along a line and sunk for later retrieval.

## The Moral Issue

Hardy not only provides an accurate description of the mechanics of smuggling he also neatly explores and summarises the moral issues. The cargoes, which come from France, are paid for beforehand and the men who unload and

The Sailor's Return at Chaldon Herring is a quintessential former smugglers' pub.

carry the goods are also paid in advance. Lizzie and Jim
Owlett, together with a couple of financial backers, make their
money from subsequent sales of the spirits. They are also the
ones who lose most if barrels are seized by Revenue Men.

The smugglers' pub served as meeting place, recruitment centre, secret storage facility, distribution depot and valued customer.

Lizzie makes the point to Stockdale that the welfare of the
village depends on free trading. She would be unable to look
after her elderly, infirm mother if she stopped smuggling and
challenges the minister:

> *'Why should you side with men who take from country
> traders what they have honestly bought wi' their own money
> in France?' she said firmly.*
> *'They are not honestly bought' said he.*
> *They are', she contradicted. 'I and Mr Owlett and the others
> paid thirty shillings for every one of the tubs before they were
> put on board at Cherbourg, and if a king who is nothing to
> us sends his people to steal our property we have a right to
> steal it back again.'*

Despite his disapproval Stockdale still accompanies his love on subsequent nightly escapades to see she comes to no harm, but it would be impossible for him to marry someone involved in illegal activity. All he demands is that she give it up. Her reasons for refusing to do so, despite the love she feels for him, also involves the excitement that livens up an otherwise dull, rural existence.

All of these arguments applied to many Dorset villages in the eighteenth and early nineteenth centuries. The taxes levied were unquestionably harsh and distribution of wealth obscenely uneven. Most of the population would have had no moral qualms about cheating the authorities, indeed the welfare of thousands depended on smuggling.

## Hide and Seek

Throughout smuggling communities contraband was not hidden only in churches but in a variety of ingenious locations and Hardy lists:

> *'hollow trees, potato-graves, fuel-houses, bedrooms, apple-lofts, cupboards, clock-cases, chimney-flues, rainwater-butts, pigsties, culverts, hedgerows, faggot-ricks, haystacks, coppers and ovens.'*

In the story Nether-Moynton is raided by zealous Customs' Officer Latimer and his team. Much of the search of the village is conducted by the men on their hands and knees. They even resort to sniffing the villagers clothing because smugglers garments often became tainted with the smell of spirits that oozed between the staves of the barrels. Hardy tells us they sniffed at:

> *'smock-frocks, old shirts and waistcoats, coats and hats, breeches and leggings, women's shawls and gowns, smith's and shoemaker's aprons, knee-naps and hedging gloves, tarpaulins, market-cloaks and even scarecrows'.*

> 'And as soon as the midday meal was over, they pushed their search into places where the spirits might have been thrown away in alarm: horse-ponds, stable drains, cinder-heaps, mixens, wet ditches, cesspools, sinks in yards, road-scrapings and back-door gutters.'

The most ingenious hiding place discovered was a subterranean vault in Owlett's orchard whose entrance had been skilfully disguised. At this point the story might be regarded as farce but, in a preface to *Wessex Tales*, Hardy assures us it is true:

> 'Among the many devices for concealing smuggled goods in caves and pits of earth, that of planting an apple tree in a tray or box which was placed over the mouth of the pit is, I believe unique, and it is detailed in "The Distracted Preacher" precisely as described by an old carrier of 'tubs' – a man who was afterwards in my father's employ for over thirty years.'

## Rescue of the Seized Contraband

At the end of two days' intensive searching Latimer's team discovers all the tubs but the men of the village cannot be found. Having disabled all the available carts, they hide at the top of the church tower from where they can monitor events.

However, the sabotage only delays the inevitable. When the transport wagons are finally repaired and loaded the Preventive Men depart for the Customs House at Budmouth (Weymouth) but are ambushed en route by a gang of heavily disguised, club wielding villagers; all with blackened faces and some dressed as women.

In the history of smuggling there are a number of instances of smugglers using force to retrieve seized goods. Hardy's story doesn't reveal the increasing use of violence in these encounters. In *The Distracted Preacher* the villagers recover their goods and merely tie up the Preventive Men who are unharmed.

This was by no means always the case in real life. Although law enforcement officers often offered little resistance to large gangs of smugglers, instances of violence occurred and there were some fierce battles like the one at Mudeford Quay, Christchurch in 1784 and the clash at Hooks Wood on Cranborne Chase in 1799 (see page 81).

Some fierce battles took place between smugglers and men from the Preventive Services.

In Kinson churchyard is the grave of Robert Trotman, leader of a local smuggling gang, shot on the shore near Poole in 1765. The inscription (now illegible) implied a ruthless action by Revenue Men and it is clear the smugglers did not think of smuggling tea they had paid for as a crime.

The grave of smuggler Robert Trotman can still be seen in Kinson churchyard although the inscription is now illegible.

However, reports of the incident show it was the smugglers who initiated the violence. Three Revenue Men were injured before any shots were fired. Interestingly, two smugglers found themselves on the jury at the inquest which ruled that Trotman had been murdered; a clear indication that public sympathy rested firmly with the smugglers.

The story of *The Distracted Preacher* has a predictable ending with Lizzie giving up smuggling in order to marry the minister. Writing in 1912, three decades after the story was published, Hardy provided an interesting footnote explaining he was constricted by English magazine conventions of the time and would have preferred a different ending which:

> '...*corresponds more closely with the true incidents. Lizzie did not, in fact, marry the minister. But – much to her credit in the author's opinion – stuck with Jim the smuggler, and emigrated with him after their marriage, an expatrial step rather forced upon him by his antecedents. They both died in Wisconsin between 1850 and 1860.*'

## Smugglers' Pubs

Reference to coaching inns, pubs, taverns and illegal drinking dens can be found throughout Thomas Hardy's novels and short stories. However, with *The Distracted Preacher*, he had an issue of credibility because neither of his main characters – a Methodist minister and a respectable young widow – would have frequented taverns or alehouses where smugglers conducted their business. This would have been the role of Lizzie's cousin Jim Owlett.

The nerve centre of smuggling operations was predominantly the local pub, where plots were hatched, arrangements for transportation agreed and runs commissioned. The smugglers' pub served as meeting place, recruitment centre, secret storage facility, distribution depot and valued customer.

The real life Owermoigne smugglers met in the *Sailors' Return* at Chaldon Herring and at the pub in Osmington Mills, now known as *The Smuggler's Inn*. These wonderful old buildings with their low-beamed ceilings, flagstone floors, inglenook fireplaces and secret hiding places are where, with a little imagination, one can sense the desperate days of smuggling's golden era.

## Abbotsbury
## **The Ilchester Arms**

9 Market Street, Abbotsbury, Weymouth DT3 4JR

Tel: 01305 871243

www.theilchester.co.uk

Eight miles northwest of Weymouth, the pretty linear village of Abbotsbury, with its golden-coloured thatched cottages, lies settled among hills behind the Fleet Lagoon and the great pebble beach of Chesil Bank. For the enterprising smuggler Abbotsbury had everything he could desire; an ideal landing beach, good storage opportunities and the perfect lookout and signalling station of St Catherine's Chapel overlooking the Fleet Lagoon.

In November 1720 fishermen from Abbotsbury made an unusual catch a mile offshore which sparked a remarkable chain of events culminating in a question being asked in parliament. Twenty-three ankers of brandy and two barrels of wine which had been *'moored with ropes'* and sunk, were brought ashore and stored in the house of Mr Whitteridge, the local Excise Officer.

This stunning view of Abbotsbury reveals itself on the journey east from Burton Bradstock along the beautiful B3157 coast road.

The old inn retains many original features and the pleasing mix of furniture styles provides a very homely experience.

Lord of the Manor, Thomas Strangeways, claimed he was entitled to the goods as part of his manorial rights and instructed his bailiff William Bradford to seize the casks and secure them under lock and key. The Collector of Customs at Weymouth, ordered William Taylor, a young Customs Officer at Abbotsbury, to retrieve the wine and spirits. Taylor failed when obstructed by a gang of locals employed by Thomas Strangeways. Eventually Taylor called for assistance from Dragoons stationed at Dorchester.

Arriving soldiers managed to recover the goods despite being confronted by a hostile, vociferous crowd. Strangeways still refusing to accept defeat claimed the casks were not contraband but salvage from a shipwreck. He protested to the Secretary of War about the use of troops and even managed to persuade an MP friend to raise the matter in the House of Commons but all to no avail.

Seventeen years later the actions of a group of Abbotsbury smugglers came to light at Bexington, on the Swyre Road,

With its portico and coaching arch, the extensive façade of The Ilchester Arms, stretches along the west side of Market Street.

The perfect lookout and signalling station of St Catherine's Chapel overlooks Fleet Lagoon and the smugglers' landing ground of Chesil Beach.

where three quarters of a ton of tea was found under hedges, along with brandy, rum, silk, cotton, and handkerchiefs.

Between 1782 and 1853 Abbotsbury smugglers who spent time in Dorchester Gaol included fishermen James Hurden (thirty-one) and Thomas Ferry (nineteen), who both served three months imprisonment having failed to raise the £100 optional fine – equivalent to more than a year's wages.

Others caught and convicted were Henry Angel (sixty-six), William Roper (fifty-two), John Gee (fifty), Martha Gee (fifty-eight – who was sentenced to nine months hard labour), John Hall (twenty-one), John Crew (twenty-nine), Moses Cousins (twenty-three) and William Boatswain (twenty-six). It was the second time Boatswain had been caught. John Hall and John Crew both received death sentences for *'Assaulting and obstructing Customs officers'* but these were later commuted to two years hard labour.

As a lad, barman Sam Freeman and his mates used to explore the nearby smugglers' caves down Red Lane.

The spacious rear dining room has a welcoming contemporary feel.
**Below:** The conservatory restaurant and adjoining beer garden provide views across to St Catherine's Chapel high on its hill.

Previously called The Ship, this rambling stone-built pub was the local centre for smuggling operations during the golden age of free trading. In the nineteenth-century the building was expanded to become The Ilchester Arms, with a roadside façade extending along the west side of Market Street. In March 1808 it was the venue of a feast for the entire village then around 1000 people, to celebrate the twenty first birthday of the then Earl of Ilchester. There is no mention of how or where they obtained the drink for the party but it is unlikely it would have presented a problem.

By 1889 when it first appeared as The Ilchester Arms it had developed into a coaching inn. Many original features remain including the large coaching arch, interior floors of quarry tiles and bare boards and heavy oak beamed ceilings.

The furniture is a pleasant jumble of old and new with pine and white painted tables and

The twelfth-century Abbotsbury tithe barn, where contraband was formerly hidden, is now part of a Children's Adventure Farm. **Inset:** Inside the tithe barn is a large replica of a smugglers' lugger and a Revenue Cutter where children can play plus a statue of smuggling chief Isaac Gulliver and two educational display boards.

Smugglers' cottages at the entrance of Red Lane opposite the village stores.

**Right:** Red Lane leads immediately into the countryside providing access to sandstone caves (now hidden in undergrowth) formerly used by Abbotsbury smugglers as first stage storage for contraband.

chairs with comfortable chesterfield leather sofas and wingback armchairs. The decoration, including the lighting, is quirky and amusingly informal, reflecting the landlord's previous life as a film cameraman.

Besides the large bar there are spacious dining areas, one with the homely presence of an upright piano. The conservatory restaurant and adjoining beer garden provide views across to St Catherine's Chapel high on its hill. This classic reminder of eighteenth-century stagecoach days continues to function as an inn with ten bedrooms to choose from.

## Bere Regis
**The Drax Arms**

West Street, Bere Regis BH20 7HH

Tel: 01929 471386

www.thedraxarms.co.uk

Situated 6 miles northeast of Wareham, Bere Regis, for its diminutive size and relative isolation is one of the most interesting Dorset villages. The first syllable 'Bere' has nothing to do with our favourite amber liquid. Instead it is Saxon meaning a scrub, copse, bramble or thorn-bed. The Regis, or Royal connection, dates from the first Saxon Queen Elfrida who, in 979 fled here from Corfe Castle suspected of murdering her stepson Edward the Martyr. In 1209, having given up an attempt to invade the coast of Normandy, King John came to reside here and is thought to have built the 'must see' historic church, from monies extracted from his subjects.

The annual five day fair held at the top of Woodbury Hill, half a mile northwest of the village, was once the largest in England. It flourished for a number of years before receiving an official charter in 1216 during the reign of Henry III. At this time a certain John de Turberville is found paying an annual fee in respect of some land in the forest of Bere.

Architectural clues suggest The Drax Arms in West Street Bere Regis dates from at least the seventeenth century.

In Thomas Hardy's *Wessex Novels*, particularly *Tess of the D'Urbervilles*, Bere and its nearby hilltop fairground feature as *Kingsbere-sub-Greenhill*, the:

> 'half-dead townlet ... the spot of all spots in the world which could be considered the D'Urbervilles' home, since they had resided there for full five hundred years.'

The Drax Arms is a proper village local where customers are welcome to pop in for a pint and a chat.

Hardy's fictionalised *D'Urberville* family was based on imagined impoverished descendants of the real life Turberville family who had been lords of the manor here for 500 years. A couple of particularly poignant scenes in the novel are set in the churchyard and church of St John the Baptist. It is possible Hardy had The Drax Arms in mind as the inn where Alec D'Urberville stayed.

Throughout the smuggling era Bere Regis was generally a somnolent place falling gradually into decay through lack of interest and funding from the Turbervilles. Henry Drax bought the Bere Regis estate from the surviving Turbervilles in 1733 but was equally uninterested in cottage repairs when rent returns were so low; consequently some of the older properties simply collapsed. Drax, who had inherited both the massive Charborough Estate in Dorset and the family's sugar-producing slave plantations in Barbados, became MP for Wareham in 1718 and for Lyme Regis in 1727.

In the twentieth century a new factor impacted on Bere Regis in the form of increasing heavy traffic along the Poole to Dorchester highway which passed through the village centre, shaking the foundations of properties along North Street. Following construction of the bypass Bere Regis is once again peaceful with the possibility once more to enjoy a quiet stroll while appreciating the abundance of remaining listed properties including the remarkable Drax Arms.

In a letter from the Poole Customs House in 1780, when James Kitcatt was landlord of The Drax Arms, Bere Regis was described as: *'a place of resort of the most notorious and dangerous smugglers'*. One of the leading contraband traders was *'a resolute young fellow'* called Robert Gillingham.

Two years earlier, in 1778, this belligerent free trader took part in a daring rescue of brandy and rum which had been seized by Customs Officers who reported it would be: *'difficult and hazardous'* to apprehend Gillingham and his friends'. This assessment proved to be a fair judgement. More than two years later the same officers, declaring *'he will never be served'* were still trying to serve him with a writ which he flatly refused to accept.

Good traditional pub food is served daily in the bar/dining room.

Darts and skittles continue to be popular pursuits in this traditional pub.

Known Bere Regis smugglers, undoubtedly customers and suppliers of The Drax Arms, included James Totherfield, a forty-one-year-old labourer jailed for a year in 1801 on a charge of smuggling, and Richard Serjeant, a twenty-two-year-old butcher convicted in 1816 of: *'assaulting and obstructing a Customs Officer'*. At the same time, a twenty-year-old labourer, George Serjeant, *'who was rather knocked-kneed'* was also convicted. In 1830 James Lugg forty-three and his forty-two-year-old wife Elizabeth were both given a £14 fine and six days imprisonment for smuggling. Ann Maidment, a twenty-four-year-old buttoner, received a similar punishment.

Architectural clues suggest The Drax Arms dates from at least the seventeenth-century but the property can be traced with certainty back to the early eighteenth-century by referencing a combination of alehouse registers and parish rate books. From these sources it is possible to establish the names of the landlords through the century and a half when smuggling was at its most active.

At the beginning of the eighteenth century the property was known as 'Meerings', and can be traced back to William Meering and successive members of his family. In 1685 Benjamin Phippard owned the pub and is recorded as being paid for beer and the accommodation of travellers on many occasions during the succeeding twenty-six years.

Bryony Cull epitomises the relaxed atmosphere and friendly, hassle-free service.

In 1711 John Hewitt from Dorchester married Elizabeth Bartlett of Bere and from 1715 until 1732 he is listed as the innkeeper and church warden. From 1732 until 1737 we find the name of Elizabeth Hewitt, widow of John Hewitt paying rates *'for Meerings Late'*. From 1733 the Hewitts would have been paying their rates to the estate of Henry Drax.

From 1738 until 1743 the name Thomas Burt occurs in the alehouse records and in 1770, when the pub was known now as the King's Head, the landlord is recorded as William Scott who paid a one penny rate on his stock of beer until 1776.

The ancient inn has been known as The Drax Arms for more than 240 years and this name appears on the *Isaac Taylor* map of 1777 with the tenant named as James Kitcatt. Fifty-three years later the surname appears as licensee in the trade directory for 1830, and it would likely be a son or namesake. In 1842, nearing the end of the smuggling era John Vivian was the landlord superseded by James Vincent who stayed until 1852 when smuggling had all but ceased.

During the smuggling era numerous contraband convoys would have passed along this bridle path leading from Bere to Turners Puddle.

The Drax Arms has a relaxed atmosphere with a friendly, hassle-free service. It is a proper village local where one can pop in for a pint and a chat or sit down to a steak dinner with all the trimmings. Good traditional pub food is served daily in the bar/dining room, or in good weather one can take advantage of the shaded courtyard or high-level sunny beer garden.

A steep climb to the elevated beer garden is rewarded with extensive views across the Dorset countryside.

# Burton Bradstock
## Three Horseshoes

Mill Street, Burton Bradstock DT6 4QZ

Tel: 01308 897259

www.threehorseshoesburtonbradstock.co.uk

Burton Bradstock is situated approximately 2½ miles south-east of Bridport and half a mile inland from the coast. This charming example of a Dorset village lies in the Bride Valley, where the small river sparkles past the church on its way to the sea. The compact community comprises a wealth of sixteenth- and seventeenth-century thatched cottages, all of which would once have provided homes for farming and fisher folk involved in smuggling.

In 1776 Isaac Gulliver bought land north of Burton Bradstock including Eggardon Farm and the Iron Age fort of Eggardon Hill. He famously planted a grove of pine trees on the summit to act as a seamark for his incoming luggers. Some of the vessels headed for a gap in the cliffs which forms Burton Bradstock's Hive Beach.

Formerly called The Ship Inn the pub was renamed The Three Horseshoes when a blacksmith/farrier moved in to the adjacent lean-to workshop.

Contraband runs were planned and instructions passed on in one or other of the pubs. Having received their orders broad backed men and experienced horse handlers assembled at an appointed time within the sound of waves breaking on Hive Beach. Anxious landsmen and mariners on an incoming vessel looked to the clifftop for any sign of a fire, warning the run was called off for that night because Customs Men were patrolling in the vicinity.

Safely landed contraband was transported inland up a track leading to Burton Bradstock village. Local pubs would be supplied with spirits and tobacco before the convoys moved further inland. In a couple of miles the trail becomes an undulating twisting country lane snaking through Shipton Gorge. Evidence of Isaac Gulliver's presence is recognised today in the names of some of the properties.

The Three Horseshoes c1900 showing the former adjacent shop and Mrs Samways, the landlady at the pub door.

Burton Bradstock's Hive Beach and its women smugglers are mentioned in an 1804 report from the Customs House at Weymouth:

*'The articles generally smuggled from this part of the coast are chiefly brandy, rum and Geneva (gin), to which may be*

added a small quantity of wine, tobacco and salt, the whole from the islands of Guernsey and Alderney, which are imported in casks containing from four to six gallons each in vessels from ten to thirty tons burthen in the winter, and in the summer season in boats from three to eight or nine tons carrying three hundred and fifty casks, which are generally sunk on rafts till a convenient opportunity offers for taking them up, which they put into boats and distribute them along the coast at Portland and on the beach called Chiswell Beach as far west as Burton Hive, which is about sixteen miles in extent. It then gets into the hands of women and others, who disperse it in small quantities in the country for five or six miles round.'

In 1940 Walter Cliff (centre) was the landlord.

There is no difficulty in imagining the likes of farm labourer John Groves, and his fishermen friends Thomas Parsons and George Gerrard drinking in the bar of the Three Horseshoes while discussing their next smuggling run. In 1816 Groves was convicted of *'making a light and fire as a signal to person or persons in smuggling vessel'*. Parsons and Gerrard were convicted of *'obstructing Customs officers'*. All three were given sentences of six months hard labour.

An early survey of the Three Horseshoes referred to some original seventeenth-century windows. Later, in 1965 when the pub was re-thatched, some of the rafters were revealed to be ash poles, cut straight from woodland and ships masts.

This three-hundred-year-old pub was formerly known as The Ship Inn. Later it was owned by the Bristol brewers Georges Ltd., who changed the name to the Three Horseshoes when a blacksmith/farrier moved in to the adjacent lean-to workshop. At this time the pub occupied only the right hand part of the present building. The left side became home to the old village post office and stores. When Palmers, the Bridport brewers, purchased the business they acquired the adjoining shop enabling them to extend and refurbish the pub.

Benches in front of the pub are perfect for relaxing on a sunny day.

**Below:** The cosy little dining room bar to the left of the entrance, with a woodburner in the inglenook, was originally the village shop.

MORE DORSET SMUGGLERS' PUBS

The ales are all from the local Palmers Bridport brewery.
**Below:** The stylish dining room marks the extent of the original pub the smugglers knew.

Today this attractive characterful pub is comfortable, homely, roomy and dog friendly. In the neat dining room/village bar contemporary furniture is arranged on plain boards. Stone in some of the walls has been exposed and the formerly blackened timbers have been sandblasted recently to reveal the wood's natural warm colour. Comfortable armchairs stand on a patterned rug in front of a woodburner providing winter cheer. In fine weather the beer garden is a lovely relaxing suntrap. Heaters are installed on the large partly covered terrace and there are picnic-sets on the lawn.

This painting is thought to depict Isaac Gulliver and some of his army of smugglers.

Consistently good-value classic pub meals are complemented by tempting specialities like braised lamb shank with

A gap in the cliffs formed the Hive contraband landing beach at Burton Bradstock.

pancetta and kale, mashed potato and mint gravy; Indonesian seafood curry prepared with sea bass; and tiger prawns and king scallops served with green bean and coconut salad or pilau rice. Vegetarian options include baked shallot, pear and goats cheese tart with Dorset baby leaves, roasted beetroot and walnuts.

Evidence of Isaac Gulliver's presence is still apparent today in the names of some Shipton Gorge properties.

## Cerne Abbas
### The Royal Oak
23 Long Street, Cerne Abbas DT2 7JG

Tel: 01300 341797

The Royal Oak, built in 1540 incorporates materials salvaged from the Abbey destroyed during Henry VIII's systematic suppression of Catholic monasteries.

The attractive village of Cerne Abbas with its stream and streets of ancient houses grew up around the great Benedictine Abbey founded in AD 987. The Abbey surrendered to Henry VIII in 1539 during the Dissolution of the Monasteries and was largely destroyed; though parts of the Abbot's Porch and Abbey guesthouse remain. Materials salvaged from the Abbey were used to erect new buildings in the vicinity including The Royal Oak.

The Manor of Cerne Abbas was owned by a succession of private landlords, who systematically stripped the Abbey of its materials for profit, such that a survey of the village by John Norden in 1617 found the Abbey: *'wholly ruinated'* and Cerne *'most disorderly governed'*.

In the centuries after the Dissolution, the village thrived as a small market town its wealth largely generated by brewing,

## The Royal Oak

40 yards South of the Church, was built in 1540 from the remains of the Abbey. There are some original shaped brackets supporting the roof on the North side. Inside the building, one room has original moulded ceiling beams and a cross fireplace with a four centred head. The building was originally a Coaching Inn and Blacksmiths.

A walkway passes the length of the pub with the bar to the left and a series of small open rooms on the right.

a practice initiated by the monks. The village's underground water particularly enhanced the quality of the beer, which was sold as far away as London and even exported to the Americas.

In 1747 the village supported 17 public inns and taverns, serving visitors and a resident population of about 1500. In 1754 the widely travelled Bishop Richard Pococke declared Cerne was *'more famous for beer than in any other place in this country'*. The availability of water power also provided impetus for other small industries including milling, tanning, silk weaving, glove and hat making.

One room boasts original ecclesiastical moulded ceiling beams.

Cerne Abbas today boasts a number of shops and tearooms and three remaining historic pubs; The Royal Oak, The Giant Inn (formerly the Red Lion) and The New Inn, all located in Long Street.

Prominent among Dorset merchants trading out of Weymouth in the early eighteenth century, the Randall family of Cerne Abbas occupied a warehouse abutting the market square a few steps from The Royal Oak. Enthusiastic supporters of the trade to the American colonies, they were equally in favour of the profits of smuggling tea and rum.

The Royal Oak incorporates a number of interesting alcoves and cosy corners.

Thomas Randall of Cerne ventured into the slave trade in the spring of 1717. For this he chartered a London ship, *The Flying Brigantine*, whose captain and part-owner was Stephen Patrick, an ex-company commander familiar with African

This intriguing sealed off door with its ancient lock faces in the direction of the twelfth-century St Mary's church.

Always on offer in this historic free house is Blonde Bitter from Cerne Abbas's own micro brewery.

and Caribbean waters who had delivered a consignment of African slaves to Barbados in 1709.

*The Flying Brigantine*, at barely 50 tons burden, was a relatively small ship for this type of enterprise. Randall loaded her with a considerable quantity of smuggled spirits and 6 tons of iron. Her ostensible destination was Madeira, but the presence of iron, a commodity extensively traded for human cargo, along with a substantial amount of beans, a staple food for plantation slaves, betrayed her true intent. Later that year, Captain Patrick traded seventeen Africans in Charlestown, South Carolina, presumably having delivered the majority of the slaves elsewhere, possibly Barbados. It seems the voyage was less profitable than expected so the Randalls returned to trading only colonial produce and smuggling.

The pub is popular with visitors and friendly locals.

Charles Weeks, an incorrigible local character was described as: *'a flying smuggler of no certain residence'* frequently operating in the Dorchester area. He supplied contraband to George and Thomas Randall as well as other Dorset and London based merchants. Weeks's house at Winfrith was described by Philip Taylor, Collector of Customs at Weymouth, as a *'general magazine of snuff, pepper, cocoa nuts (beans), coffee and other goods'*.

The decked garden is a welcome feature during warmer days and evenings.

In 1717, during a customs search of the village, George Randall threatened the Riding Officer with murder. The following year smuggled linen was seized at Thomas Randall's home and 20 gallons of brandy were discovered under corn in a wagon at nearby Duntish Mill.

A description of the Randall gang at work was given to Philip Taylor by Edmund Coish who lived in a part of Dorset: *'through which the smugglers' troops do frequently pass'*. Coish himself was a man of *'indifferent reputation and circumstance'* but Taylor, possibly meeting in a Cerne pub, encouraged him to talk over a drink. Taylor later wrote:

The Randall family tomb can be seen in the central aisle in St Mary's church.

*'I liquored him with October (strong beer) and plied him with the usual questions. I make to the country people of the price of wine and brandy and how they are supplied with the same, whereto he replied that there was great running in their country and the Tuesday before, soon after day, he saw between twenty and thirty men armed with clubs and staves*

In 1717 twenty gallons of brandy were discovered hidden under corn in a wagon in a mill adjacent to Duntish Mill Farm.

Parts of the Abbot's Porch and Abbey guesthouse remain.

*and other weapons come from towards Cerne, where he was told they had conducted some goods for Mr. George Randell, but in what house the same was lodged and whither it was removed thence, as usual he could not tell.'*

Although Coish claimed he didn't know where the contraband was hidden, he possibly feared the powerful Randalls.

The Royal Oak stands forty yards south of St Mary's church in the former market place. This popular thatched, partly creeper clad, village centre pub has flagstone floors and a wealth of black beams and supporting timbers. The presence of original shaped brackets supporting eaves on the north side confirm that it was built in 1540, partly with materials from the ruined Abbey.

The attractive interior is revealed in stages. A walkway passes the length of the pub with the bar to the left and a series of small open rooms on the right. One such spacious alcove boasts original ecclesiastical moulded ceiling beams and an ancient stone fireplace. Tables stand in front of the pub with more in the small back garden.

The Royal Oak has changing lunchtime and evening menus which may include Portland crab and local game. Always on offer in this historic free house is Blonde Bitter from Cerne Abbas's own micro brewery.

# Chaldon Herring
## Sailor's Return

Chaldon Herring DT2 8DN

Tel: 01305 854441

www.sailorsreturnpub.com

Between the two World Wars this tiny village 7 miles west of Weymouth became a Mecca for artists and writers. They were drawn to it not only for its beauty and tranquility but also because it was home to the remarkable author T. F. Powys whose stories explore universal themes within this microcosm of the rural world.

Chaldon Herring features as *Folly Down* in his haunting novel *Mr. Weston's Good Wine*. The title is taken from Jane Austen's *Emma*, in which Mr Weston believes that: *'There is no place in*

The Sailor's Return, originally one of a pair of solid walled, thatched cottages, has been substantially extended with new wings at both ends.

the round world provides more peace and joy to its inhabitants than this village'.

Just above the village green is the long, low, whitewashed Sailor's Return which appropriately enough appears in the story as The Angel, considering that Mr Weston's assistant is the Archangel Michael. The pub, its Landlord Thomas Bunce; *'a gentleman who, by the appearance of him, could be merry in all his parts'* and his daughter Jenny are all central to the story.

The original smugglers' bar became the heart of a former colony of writers and artists, and is featured in a number of books and stories.

The Sailor's Return has been enlarged since 1926 but Powys' description (apart from the sign) still applies today:

> 'The inn is placed upon a little hill. At its entrance is a finely painted sign board of an angel. The inn itself is covered by a good coating of thatch that is the very best straw in use in this part of the country and is called reed. The thatch keeps the house warm in winter and cool in summer, and the ale that is kept in a narrow passage between the kitchen and the parlour is by no means in a common way a bad beverage.'

One of the writers attracted to the village at that time was David Garnett who lodged in the pub and wrote an insightful

MORE DORSET SMUGGLERS' PUBS

This traditional country pub is full of evocative nooks and crannies suggestive of former smuggling days. **Below:** Later extensions to the original pub provide comfortable spacious dining areas.

novel about colour prejudice. The story, published in 1925, is called *The Sailor's Return* and is set at the end of the golden age of smuggling in the summer of 1858. It was the first significant work in British literature to feature a black female as a major character.

*The small fresh menu focused on local, seasonal produce is very popular with families.*

In the story retiring English sea captain, William Targett, returns from a voyage to western Africa and rents a pub in a sleepy Dorset village. Here the former mariner sets about building a life for his African princess bride Tulip and their son Olu, but local residents, and even his own relatives have other ideas. It is a compelling tale that, once read, is never forgotten.

*The Sailor's Return is a free house offering a range of West Country ales plus Dorset cider from Lulworth.*

Given the parish topography and its close proximity to other notorious smuggling villages it is not surprising that Chaldon Herring is famed for the free trading families of Stickland, Squibb and Snelling. These country folk who frequented the pub and supplied the landlord with duty free goods were mentioned regularly in the registers of Dorchester Gaol.

Chaldon Herring lies halfway between the contraband landing beaches around Lulworth and the inland village of Owermoigne, the setting for Thomas Hardy's definitive smuggling tale *The Distracted Preacher*. Contraband landed at the coast was conveyed through Chaldon Herring and Owermoigne on its way to markets at Sherborne and Yeovil.

Extremely sheltered, Lulworth Cove could be used virtually in all weathers by the smugglers of Chaldon Herring and

The extremely sheltered Lulworth Cove could be used virtually in all weathers by the smugglers of Chaldon Herring and Owermoigne.

Owermoigne and was an ideal spot to sink tubs. In 1719 around a dozen smugglers were stopped in the early hours of a summer's morning near Lulworth Cove attempting to run a shipment of wine and brandy. They fought like demons with flails, swords and clubs, but when it appeared the cache would be lost the smugglers staved in some of the barrels and carried off the remainder. The battle between smugglers and Revenue Men continued for some twelve hours, and attracted people from four parishes who hastened away with the abandoned contraband.

Confirmation that local smugglers took every opportunity not to be identified by Customs Men is borne out by a tombstone inscription in Weymouth's Bury Street cemetery which reads:

> *'Sacred to the memory of Lieut Thos Edward Knight, RN, of Folkestone, Kent, Aged 42, who in the execution of his duty as Chief Officer of the Coastguard was wantonly attacked by a body of smugglers near Lulworth on the night of 28th of June 1832, by whom after being unmercifully beaten he was thrown over the cliff near Durdle Door from the effects of which he died the following day.'*

The Sailor's Return was originally a pair of solid walled thatched cottages built in the old Dorset fashion using stone and rubble, and originally included a pre-reformation altar stone amongst its flagstones. Nestled in the tranquil village of Chaldon Herring this traditional country pub is full of evocative nooks and crannies suggestive of former smuggling days.

The present landlord Tom Brachi and his team confidently achieve their stated goal of maintaining a traditional bar atmosphere, alongside a cosy restaurant offering a small fresh menu based on local seasonal produce. Unsurprisingly it is often described as a gem of a pub.

*In 1832 Coastguard Officer Edward Knight was thrown over the cliffs at Durdle Door by local smugglers fearful of being identified.*

## Chideock
### George Inn

Main Street, Chideock DT6 6JD

Tel: 01297 489419

www.georgeinnchideock.co.uk

Chideock is a rural village boasting several old thatched cottages situated approximately 2.5 miles west of Bridport and 5 miles east of Lyme Regis on the A35. It is less than a mile inland from Seatown on the Jurassic Coast World Heritage Site.

Much of the surviving information on smuggling at Chideock and Seatown comes from notes made by Reverend C. V. Goddard, vicar in Charmouth during the nineteenth century. Although once widespread, smuggling on the south west

The inn sign depicts George II at the battle of Dettingen in Germany in June 1743. This was the last battle in which an English king took part.

coast by then had mostly ceased. The Reverend found many of his parishioners had formerly been engaged in the illicit trade, and he wrote a record of their experiences.

Apparently nearly everyone in Chideock had been involved to a greater or lesser extent, with the local families of Bartletts, Farewells, Oxenburys and Orchards leading the way. Rev'd Goddard's church warden, Sam Bartlett, having been brought up in the smuggling trade was a useful source of information.

The Chideock gang was led by a former army officer known simply as 'the Colonel'. He specialised in the use of pack-horses, uncommon along this part of the coast. His gang landed goods between Charmouth and Seatown, marking the hills above their favoured landfalls with copses of trees in the same way Isaac Gulliver had marked Eggardon Hill. These were established on strategic prominences at Charmouth, Seatown, Eype's Mouth and Stanton St Gabriel.

The smugglers' main landing beaches were at Cain's Folly, just east of Charmouth and St Gabriel's Mouth, under the western flank of Golden Cap.

Fronting the A35 trunk road, The George Inn has been serving locals and travellers since 1685.

As with other Dorset coastal villages smugglers used local hiding places to store goods prior to onward transportation. Village Riding Officer Samuel Dawson discovered a secret room under the floor of James Gerrard's living quarters at Chideock Mill. When Dawson searched the premises in 1820 he found two casks of brandy and two of Geneva gin. The underhand Gerrard tried putting the blame on his servant boy, Samuel Long alias Dido claiming he was: *'in the habit of going down to the beach to fetch tubs continually'*, and that a day or two earlier, he had said to him: *'That's a really good place to*

Until the twentieth century the George Inn was a small cottage pub. Cromwell's troops stayed in the orchard at the back on their way to desecrate the church.

To the left of the front entrance the cosy dining area with its attractive fireplace is the original room smugglers would have known.

The present stylish and comfortable dining room.

**Right:** The team at the George Inn go out of their way to be family and dog friendly.

*hide tubs, master. The officers will never find them there'*. James's brother Anthony also lived in the house and upon hearing of the discovery claimed he: *'went away into the country'* thus exonerating Dido.

The Colonel had several local customers but was more interested in moving the contraband well inland. His preferred route passed through the Marshwood Vale and along the valley of the little River Char. Goods were delivered to regular customers in small manor houses en route and at the market towns of Beaminster and Broadwindsor. His packhorse train would then continue into Somerset, calling at Crewkerne, Chard and Yeovil itself.

Rev. Goddard's notes date the last Chideock run as late as 1882. It was led by the sixty-nine-year-old veteran smuggler Sam Bartlett and began with the customary exchange of signals with a French vessel hovering off the coast. All was well as the Chideock smugglers set off by boat from Seatown to collect their tubs. Unfortunately the transfer took longer than expected and with daybreak came the danger of Coastguard patrols.

A main feature of the George Inn is the large horseshoe shaped central bar.

After delaying a while the boat approached the shore at Eype's Mouth, where the land smugglers were anxiously watching and waiting. One of the gang perched on the cliff lost his footing and fell, colliding with a colleague and scarring him for life. A few tubs were landed before the patrol was spotted and the alarm raised. Some smugglers decided to open a tub that was otherwise at risk of being seized but one died from the effect of drinking undiluted spirit. The remaining undaunted free traders put to sea again and sank the tubs off Seatown.

Months passed before another opportunity for a run presented itself. This time an attempt was made at Burton Bradstock, but the surf was running high and no boat could go in or out. A few tubs were landed and removed by wagon through a potato field, but half of the original cargo remained at sea. Another landing was attempted below Thorncombe Beacon but the Preventive Men were alerted. The boat's tackle became tangled and the tubs were dumped back in the sea once more. Some days passed before the tubs were raised yet again. This time the chosen spot was the sluices of Bridport Harbour (later known as West Bay). A few more tubs were carried ashore before Preventives intervened and once more the boat put to sea. Eventually the small craft made its way to Abbotsbury where, at last, the final part of the cargo was landed. So ended Chideock's last run and, almost certainly, the last significant attempt to import illegally good French brandy into Dorset. It had taken six months, three sinkings and five landing attempts.

*All cask ales served in the George Inn are from the award winning Palmers Brewery in Bridport, a short distance away.*

The A35 is one of the most historic routes in Southern England originally connecting the three significant seaports of Folkestone in Kent through Southampton in Hampshire to Exeter in Devon. Fronting this ancient route, and serving locals and travellers alike since 1685, is the heavily thatched George Inn.

Early in the twentieth century, as motor cars and west country holidays became popular the original cottage pub was extended to incorporate the adjacent building and was later further extended at the rear. A recent complete refurbishment has raised the levels of style and comfort expected of a very modern pub.

The smugglers' main landing beaches were at Cain's Folly, just east of Charmouth, and St Gabriel's Mouth, under the western flank of Golden Cap itself.

The dark beamed lounge bar with its wooden floor, attractive fireplace, plush wall seats and informal dining tables is where smugglers would have combined business with pleasure. The George today is a family friendly, dog friendly pub with a sizeable horseshoe shaped central bar and three large dining areas.

On offer is a really good choice of food from light bites to huge rib-eye steaks with all the trimmings plus at least four imaginative daily specials. Available on tap is the full range of Palmers beers.

## Corfe Castle
### The Greyhound Inn

The Square, Corfe Castle BH20 5EZ

Tel: 01929 480205

www.greyhoundinn.co.uk

Sir Frederick Treves passed this way on his bicycle tour of the county a decade before the First World War. In his subsequent *Highways and Byways of Dorset* he described Corfe village as: '*A wrinkled old place in the winter of its age, lying at the foot of its castle like a faithful hound*'. This once could have applied equally and literally to the ancient Greyhound Inn (possibly England's most photographed pub) except today the Greyhound is vibrant with a new lease of life.

Standing on a natural mound in a conspicuous break midway along the Purbeck Hills the great Norman castle dominates the scene. It is now a deserted ruin, though spectacular and virtually unparalleled.

Contender for the most photographed Dorset pub, The Greyhound Inn enjoys the dramatic backdrop of ruined Corfe Castle.

Three miles south of Corfe Castle is a fault in the line of cliffs west of St Alban's Head. Contraband landed below at Chapman's Pool was carried north through Kingston to hiding places on Corfe Common and in the village itself. St Alban's Head, crested by a Norman chapel, projects a mile out into the Channel and was a perfect signalling station for smuggling vessels hovering off the coast. The question naturally arises: how could such a strangely outstanding place as Corfe Castle so strategically located avoid being a store for contraband?

In the evening of Tuesday 11 October 1774 John Wesley the founder of Methodism, came to Corfe Castle and *'preached in a meadow near the town to a deeply attentive congregation, gathered from all parts of the island'*. He described part of the ruins on the southwest side *'being fitted up with some rooms and laid out in a little garden'*. A story about the rector of Corfe living in these rooms concerns a visit from Wesley who had heard the

Sir Frederick Treves cycled to Corfe a decade before the First World War and described his impressions in *Highways and Byways of Dorset*.

63

MORE DORSET SMUGGLERS' PUBS

The pub is a very popular pit-stop for families visiting the castle.
**Below:** The Greyhound Inn comprises an interesting series of up-along-down-along dining areas.

rector was contraband controller for the Isle of Purbeck and had come to persuade him to give up free trading and concentrate on his rightful pastoral duties.

Captain Warren Lisle of Weymouth Custom House owed several of his bigger seizures to William Benfield, an informer from Corfe Castle village who passed on information about imminent arrivals of smuggling vessels heading for St Alban's Head, Ringstead or other places along the Purbeck coast. He sent his messages via Edward Thorne, the Osmington Riding Officer but in 1756 complained he had not been paid the financial rewards he had been promised.

In 1803, Thomas Keats, a stone cutter from Corfe was convicted of smuggling and spent eight months in Dorchester Gaol before his £20 fine was paid, suggesting he had help from outside. Gaoled Smugglers often hoped their fines would be paid – or at the very least their prison diet supplemented – by their free trading friends.

John Edmunds, a young sawyer from Corfe Castle was not so lucky. In 1817 the seventeen year old was convicted of smuggling and unable to pay the fine. It's hard to imagine the effect

People watching from tables in front of the pub is a popular pastime.

Among the interesting range of well-kept ales are always examples from west-country brewers.

of incarceration on a young lad used to an active outdoor life. The stress of the trauma eventually persuaded him to make a deal with the Board of Customs by trading friends' names for his own freedom.

Edmunds *'a novice in the art of smuggling'* had been summoned from his bed by one of the Corfe gang and agreed to carry some tubs. When caught in the act by Customs Men, he

The contraband landing beach at Chapman's Pool by the fault in the line of cliffs west of St Alban's Head.

dropped the goods and ran but was recognised and later picked up. He received a message promising support from others of the gang if he kept quiet, but was still waiting five months later.

In 1822 William Grant, a thirty-five-year-old Corfe labourer was convicted of smuggling but discharged after one month. Presumably he also had friends to pay his fine. In 1834 two

Eighteenth-century smugglers conveyed contraband such as fine French brandy and ladies' silk gloves across Corfe Common on their way from the Purbeck coast to London.

twenty-five-year-old men, bricklayer William Short and wheelwright Joseph Luther, were simultaneously condemned to death for: *'Unlawfully assembling armed for an illegal purpose'*. In both cases their sentences were commuted to twelve months hard labour. In the same year the Tolpuddle Martyrs were transported to Australia, essentially for meeting to discuss their plight resulting from the gradual lowering of their agricultural wages.

Treves gives this description of the exterior of The Greyhound Inn: *'The inn has a porch with a small room over it, like a miniature house. This chamber is held up, with no little dignity, by three stone pillars, which have in their time afforded comforting support to the backs of many carters while they drank their cyder.'*

The large sun-drenched garden affords excellent views of the Castle.

Steps and corridors entice the visitor through three small low-ceilinged, panelled rooms of this bustling old pub, in the centre of what is now a tourist village. The large sun-drenched garden affords excellent views of the Castle and the steam railway. There is also a pretty courtyard opening on to the castle bridge.

The Greyhound Inn is a family-friendly place with a good culinary choice ranging upwards from sandwiches and pizzas. The kitchen's priority for fresh seasonal produce is presented in dishes such as hearty Dorset Game pie, and Dorset baby back ribs in sticky barbecue sauce. Among the interesting range of well-kept ales is always a selection from west country brewers with local cider from Stoford Press.

This painting by Ernest Haslehust shows Corfe as the smugglers would have known it.

Corscombe
**The Fox Inn**
Court Hill, Corscombe, Dorchester DT2 0NS
Tel: 01935 892381
www.foxinncorscombe.com

Approximately 8 miles south-southwest of the Somerset town of Yeovil, Corscombe village is approached along sunken lanes and hollows on the northern scarp of the Dorset Downs. The name Corscombe derives from 'Corfwedges Cumb', meaning valley of the pass roads.

In 1776 Isaac Gulliver's realm had extended as far as West Dorset. At this time his favourite landing places were the gravelly beaches of Burton Bradstock, Swyre and Bexington 12 miles due south of Corscombe.

In a lovely country setting just outside the village, roses grow around the door of this picturesque mid seventeenth-century inn.

Dogs and walkers are welcome in the flagstone bar.

**Right:** The room to the left of the entrance with its inglenook, barrel furniture and curved settle conveys a very traditional impression.

Born and raised in Corscombe, Landlord Shane Childs runs the pub with his wife Marie. The cheeky apprentice is their son Thomas.

Using carts, pack-ponies and tub men free traders transported contraband goods inland through Puncknowle, Powerstock, over Toller Down, and on through Corscombe and Halstock to be delivered to eager customers in thriving, fashionable Bath and the great City of Bristol. Corscombe village and The Fox Inn marked the halfway point between the coast and Yeovil, providing a perfect, secluded resting place for tired men and ponies.

Formerly a smugglers' trail, the footpath immediately beside the pub leads to Court Farm House and the nearby property of Woodwalls, which has been extended from an original small gamekeeper's cottage. In Isaac Gulliver's time part of the cottage was used as a school and the schoolmistress's husband was an active ally of the smugglers.

The cottagey feel of the pub continues in the dining room which opens into a conservatory extension overlooking a sunken garden. **Below:** The small stream across the road from the pub completes the beautiful setting.

For busy summer weekends there are additional seats across a quiet lane by the small stream.

This enterprising gamekeeper involved his wife's pupils in digging a number of pits in the woods, traces of which can still be seen. When filled with contraband the holes were covered over with undergrowth. It is not recorded whether the pupils were paid, but years later, a nephew of one of these junior labourers recalled his uncle telling how he used to wheel away barrow-loads of earth from the excavations.

Gulliver's contraband carriers came from all parts of the county and beyond. One, Anthony Garland, was from Corscombe itself. He was apprehended in 1725 by the Lyme Regis Customs Men when riding a black mare carrying: '1¼ cwt of French salt and 1 cask brandy and strong water (diluted brandy)'.

Running immediately beside the pub, a former smugglers' trail now a footpath, leads to Court Farm House and Woodwalls.

The mid seventeenth-century Fox Inn is a traditional family run, thatched pub in a tranquil country setting just outside the village. With roses round the front door, beamed interior rooms with flagstone floors and log fires all help to provide a genuine impression of a former rustic smugglers' den.

In the room to the left are built-in settles either side of the large inglenook, with rustic stools and tables fashioned from barrels together with an assortment of country style furniture and a slate-topped bar. The cottagey feel continues in the dining room which opens into a flower-filled conservatory overlooking a sunken garden. For busy summer weekends there are additional seats across a quiet lane by a small stream.

Excavated pits, formerly used as contraband hiding places, in the woods behind Woodwalls.

Woodwalls Cottage, where in Gulliver's time, local children received a basic education from the gamekeeper's wife.

Among the tempting dishes on offer are homemade shortcrust pies served with mash, peas and gravy; pan fried whole mackerel in lemon and herb butter and linguini in a creamy broccoli and blue vinny sauce. The Fox Inn's free house status ensures an interesting variety of ales permanently on tap.

Corscombe village children helped excavate pits to conceal contraband.

## Farnham
### The Museum
Farnham, Near Blandford Forum  DT11 8DE

Tel: 01725 516261

www.museuminn.co.uk

Formerly known as The Old Ash Inn, there are records of pubs like this being used as temporary hospitals and mortuaries following battles between smugglers and soldiers.

Seven miles northeast of Blandford Forum, the quiet village of Farnham lies in a dell among downs on Cranborne Chase. Today this is a peaceful, picturesque village, where white, predominantly thatched cottages nestle around the ancient church; but it hasn't always been so tranquil.

Over many centuries kings and nobles came to this area for sport. During the smuggling era Cranborne Chase was a rough wilderness and a refuge for poachers, fugitives and criminals. A number of smugglers lived here whilst others dropped off contraband on their way inland from the coast.

In March 1779 on the western edge of the village a famous battle between smugglers and Dragoons took place at Hooks

The Victorian extension created by General Pitt-Rivers to accommodate visitors to his museum.

The bar of the old pub with its low ceilings, flagstone floors and a roaring log fire, has a cosy, traditional feel.

Wood, which was vividly described in a contemporary newspaper report:

'The Excise Officer at Cranborne, having intelligence of upwards of 20 horses, loaded with smuggled goods, passing by that place he with six dragoons, quartered in Cranborne, armed with guns, swords, pistols etc., went in pursuit of them and, about 4 o'clock in the afternoon, finding the goods in a coppice near Hooks Wood in the parish of Farnham, they immediately seized them, loaded their horses and began to carry them away; upon which the smugglers, who were not too far distant collected themselves to the number of 40 or 50 and attacked the dragoons in order to rescue their goods, when a fray ensued.'

'The soldiers with their broad swords behaved with great resolution and bravery. The Exciseman, it is said, fired his fusse and wounded one of the smugglers in the arm, so that it must be amputated. Another smuggler was shot in the left breast, and the ball went through him. The smugglers made use of large clubs and being highly exasperated dealt their *blows about very severely. They were at last victorious. They beat the soldiers in an inhuman manner, broke their swords, demolished their firearms and carried off their horses in triumph, but they [the horses] have all since been found.'*

One of the stylish dining room areas in the extension wing.

Two smugglers were arrested the next morning at an inn on the Blandford Road. This may well have been The Blacksmith's Arms at Thorney Down owned and run by Isaac Gulliver. The lawless couple were tried at Dorset Assizes for '*taking goods from some officers of Excise*' but both were acquitted. A third smuggler died of his wounds but the remainder of the 40 or 50 involved were never identified and remained at large.

Chettle House, a mile south of Farnham, was owned at the time of the battle by a friend of Isaac Gulliver, the Reverend William Chaffin. The house is reputed to have a secret underground passage of the type used by smugglers. It was Chaffin who sold the prehistoric hill fort of Eggardon to Gulliver, who had planted a copse of trees as a sea-mark guide for the captains of his contraband vessels. William Chaffin (1733-1818), a keen hunter and shooter, wrote the best account of

The very relaxed ambience at The Museum today is a dramatic contrast to the desperate days of free traders.

the conflict between local gamekeepers and deer poachers: *Anecdotes and History of Cranborne Chase*. Chettle House remained with the Chaffin family until the death of the last of the line. In 1845 it passed into the hands of the Castleman family when Wimborne banker Edward Castleman bought it and with his wife Anne Castleman (née Gulliver), a granddaughter of the socially ambitious free trader, took up residence.

The Museum today comprises a seventeenth-century thatched country pub and a spacious Victorian red brick extension. Formerly known as The Old Ash Inn the pub was renamed in the late nineteenth century by General Pitt Rivers who inherited the Rushmore Estate in 1880. The General, whose full length portrait appears on the inn sign, had interests in archaeology and ethnology beginning in the 1850s during overseas army postings. By the time of his retirement

Dragoons stationed at Cranborne would have frequented The Old Ash Inn and tables still stand outside for alfresco drinking and dining.

FARNHAM

*The smugglers: 'beat the soldiers in an inhuman manner and carried off their horses in triumph'.*

he had amassed ethnographic collections numbering tens of thousands of items from all over the world. General Pitt Rivers established a museum on the estate to house his collection which, in its heyday, attracted twelve thousand visitors a year. It was at this time he extended the old inn to provide

*A tranquil coppice in Hooks Wood where in March 1779 a famous battle between smugglers and Dragoons took place.*

The former Blacksmith's Arms at Thorney Down owned by Isaac Gulliver, possibly where two of the smugglers were arrested on the morning following the Hooks Wood battle.

refreshments and accommodation for visitors. The Farnham Museum existed until the 1960s when the collection became part of the Oxford Museum of Natural History.

Chettle House at the time of the battle was home to Isaac Gulliver's friend Reverend William Chaffin. Gulliver's granddaughter Anne lived here after 1845.

## Fiddleford
### Fiddleford Inn
Calfclose Lane, Fiddleford DT10 2BX

Tel: 01258 472886

Fiddleford on the River Stour is a small rural community within the locality of Okeford Fitzpaine, set back from the A357, 2 miles east of Sturminster Newton and 6 west of Blandford Forum. At its northeastern edge stands the undisputed jewel in its crown, the medieval Manor completed in 1370, formerly a mill house.

In 1774, a lengthy enquiry into the state of smuggling in this part of Dorset concluded that: *'Issac Gulliver, William Beale and Roger Ridout run great quantities of goods from our North Shore between Poole and Christchurch'*. It seems that Roger Ridout, working with Isaac Gulliver, was involved with the overland transportation of contraband. The Ridout gang, who achieved legendary status in North Dorset, left the occasional nocturnal

Originally an agricultural building dating from around 1740, The Fiddleford Inn was where barley was converted into malt used in the brewing process.

Flooring in the three beamed linked areas is an effective mix of wood, carpet and old flagstones.
**Below:** Removal of sections of interior plaster has revealed original golden sandstone walls.

bribe of a keg of brandy on the doorstep of local magistrate Thomas Dashwood, who lived at Vine House in Sturminster Newton's Penny Street.

Writing in 1895, Thomas's grandson, H. C. Dashwood, gave an account of the smuggling era:

> 'My father stated that when a boy, in or about 1794, he had, when riding late at night seen the string of horses in the narrow road between Okeford Fitzpaine and Fiddleford with the kegs and other contraband goods on the horses. One or two men, armed, generally were in front and then ten or twelve horses connected by ropes or halters followed at a hard trot, and two or three men brought up the rear.'

The pub is furnished with a pleasing assortment of contemporary and traditional styles. Bench pews and pine tables share dining space with modern tables and colourful cushioned chairs.

His report paints a graphic picture of those desperate times:

> 'This cavalcade did not stop for any person, and it was very difficult to get out of their way, as the roads, until the turnpikes were made in 1724, would only allow for one carriage, except in certain places. The contraband goods were principally brought from Lulworth and the coast through White-

Fiddleford brewery was converted in the nineteenth century into a hotel known as Archway House, becoming the Fiddleford Inn in 1972.

*parish and Okeford Fitzpaine, through the paths in the woods to Fiddleford, and thus distributed.'*

Roger Ridout was born at Shroton near Blandford in 1736 and was only ten when he inherited a house and orchard near Fiddleford. Aged twenty he married Mary and moved to Fiddleford where he augmented his miller's income with proceeds from smuggling. Sometime between 1746 and 1784 he moved to The Mills on the Okeford Fitzpaine to Shillingstone road. Ridout's main contraband storage facility was Fiddleford Mill and Farm where the tenants kept the barn and stables well stocked with hay and straw for concealing the smuggled goods.

Dashwood senior may have been influential in 1781 when Roger, his wife Mary and son William – along with their friend Richard 'Ducky' Pope – were all acquitted at Dorchester Assizes of murdering Thomas Penny. However, unlike

Fiddleford Mill and outbuildings were used as temporary contraband stores by the notorious Ridout gang. **Below:** Smugglers also frequented two local ale houses: The Trout (now May Cottage) and The Bell (now The Travellers Rest).

his associate Isaac Gulliver, Roger Ridout was not always successful in evading the law. On one occasion in 1787, presumably outside Thomas Dashwood's area of jurisdiction, he was caught smuggling and spent time in Dorchester Gaol.

With a little help from his friends Roger managed to raise the £40 fine and was released within a fortnight. Ridout family folklore tells how the notorious smuggler, languishing in gaol, was fortified by Mary who walked the 40 mile round trip from Okeford Fitzpaine with a bladder of brandy concealed in her bosom. The container had a tube attached which she passed between the bars for her husband to enjoy a sly tipple.

Another story tells how Roger was challenged one day by an Excise Officer concerning the contents of a jar he was carrying home from Fiddleford Brewery. However, the jar did not contain dutiable liquor but quick-acting yeast or 'barm' which, when the cork was removed sprayed into the officer's face enabling the smuggler to push his adversary into a ditch and run off.

Roger and Mary had seven sons some of whose descendants still live in the village today. Okeford Fitzpaine's involvement in smuggling continued well into the nineteenth century when 'Ducky' Pope took over leadership of the gang.

The author standing by the grave of Roger and Mary Ridout. Mary died in 1809 and Roger two years later.

Dating from around 1740, The Fiddleford Inn was originally an agricultural building where barley was converted into malt used in the brewing process. Beer was brewed here sometime later when it became known as Adams' Brewery or Archway Brewery.

Vine House in Sturminster Newton, home of local magistrate Thomas Dashwood, where occasional kegs of brandy were left on the doorstep by grateful smugglers.

**Below:** Okeford Fitzpaine Mill.

In 1821, Philip Adams applied for a licence to *'keep a certain common inn or Alehouse at Ockford Fitzpaine known as the Travellers Rest'*. It seems possible that Philip expanded his enterprise into brewing and was followed by later generations. Kelly's Directory of Fiddleford for 1880 lists Philip Charles Adams as a brewer and maltster. Now a private house, The Travellers Rest stands a few hundred yards east along the A357 from the Fiddleford Inn.

Today the Fiddleford Inn is a welcoming, family friendly free house. Flooring in the three beamed linked areas is an effective mix of wood, carpet and old flagstones. Sections of interior plaster have been removed revealing original golden coloured sandstone walls.

The pub is furnished with a pleasing assortment of contemporary and traditional styles. Bench pews and pine tables share dining space with modern tables and colourful cushioned chairs. The relaxed, cosy atmosphere is complemented with honest pub food and a well-chosen selection of real ales. The log burner is welcoming on winter days and nights and for summer days there are picnic-sets in the large fenced garden where occasional live music can be enjoyed.

*The Ridouts lived here next to the mill when part of the building would have been used to store grain or house livestock.*

# Kingston
## Scott Arms

Kingston, Corfe Castle BH20 5LH

Tel: 01929 480270

www.thescottarms.com

The Scott Arms is named after Kingston's pre-eminent land-owning family.

Kingston is a photogenic village in a stunning setting. Ample proof lies in framed photographs of film shoots lining the corridors of the Scott Arms. There's *Hereward the Wake*, filmed in 1965; a BBC TV version of *The Three Musketeers* shot the following year and *The Mayor of Casterbridge* from 1977. In some of the photographs the actors, in spotless costumes, have shiny hair and suspicious moustaches and appear very dated and quaintly unconvincing against the authentic setting.

With popular contraband landing places nearby, Kingston was long known as a smugglers haunt. The wonderfully wild beach and secluded cove of Chapman's Pool is only one-and-

In summer and autumn Virginia creeper smothers the pub's exterior.

a-half miles south of the pub. Here a stream flows out to sea after plunging down a ravine carved through cliffs between Houns-tout and St Alban's Head. At Winspit a break in the cliffs enabled free traders with their horses to reach contraband landed on the shore.

Local smuggling legends include the story of a Swanage surgeon called upon to treat a wounded Kingston smuggler. For his own protection as well as the smuggler's he was blindfolded on the journey and therefore unable to report where he had been.

*A warm welcome accompanies a perfect selection of west-country ales.*

Another story tells of the new Customs recruit who was instructed not to allow anyone to land contraband on his

*The compact front bar has a very traditional pub atmosphere.*

The warren-like interior is full of historic interest.  **Below:** Large windows in the split level rear barn extension look out over the garden with Corfe Castle as a magnificent backdrop.

section of the coast. He thought he was doing a good job when he encountered smugglers attempting a landing and told them to move off.

There is also the early example of William Culliford of Kingston, son of Robert Culliford owner of Encombe Manor who became MP for Wareham. As a young man in 1681 William worked for the Treasury investigating frauds, corruption and Customs in South West England and South Wales. His diligent detection led to the suspension of thirty-eight Customs Officers including several at the Dorset ports of Poole, Weymouth and Lyme.

*The view of Corfe Castle from the pub garden.*

Despite this action smuggling was still rife locally nearly a century later and William Morton Pitt, who owned Encombe in the 1770s, had ambitions to steer the local population away from the illegal trade by offering alternative employment. He opened a factory making rope, twine, sackcloth, sailcloth and dowlas – a strong, closely woven, linen fabric. Although he created two hundred jobs Pitt's noble initiative was not valued and soon abandoned by the Kingston folk who returned to the lure of free trading.

Today a local walking trail called 'Smugglers' Ways' has been created following the coast path from Worth Matravers visiting places where smugglers were known to bring goods ashore. Another walking route, The Purbeck Way, leads from Wareham to Corfe Castle, then eastward to Ballard Down (near Swanage) and west along the South West Coast path to Chapman's Pool.

From the high point at Kingston, the trail heads for the sea along the crest of a high downland ridge. Here the splendid views take in one of Dorset's loveliest valleys, known as the Golden Bowl. The route continues along the dramatic cliff top of Houns-tout, overlooking the blue, scallop-shaped bay of Chapman's Pool, one of the most favoured smuggling landing places.

The Scott Arms, with its profusion of Virginia creeper in summer and autumn, is named after Kingston's pre-eminent family. John Scott, first Earl of Eldon, was the longest-ever serving Lord Chancellor, retaining the role for twenty-six years.

The clearly defined smugglers' trail leading directly from the beach at Kimmeridge Bay. The concrete blocks are part of the WWII anti-tank defences.

A row of former Coastguard cottages stands back from the smugglers' landing beaches at Kimmeridge and Worbarrow Bay.

The extensively modernised pub rambles through several levels of warren-like beamed rooms, some furnished with sofas and easy chairs. Stripped stone walls, bare boards and log fires enhance the feeling of authenticity. Summer barbecues are held in the large attractive garden with an outstanding view of Corfe Castle and the Purbeck Hills.

So spectacular is the panorama from the Scott Arms that a mounted telescope has become a permanent fixture in the beer garden. Centre stage are the shattered ruins of Corfe Castle, framed in perfect symmetry by a pair of thoughtfully matching hills. Some distance away, behind the castle, are glimpses of Poole Harbour.

Viewed through the telescope, the winding streets, rooftops and church of Corfe resemble a model town and when the steam locomotive of Swanage Railway trundles through with its shiny green carriages in tow the impression is complete.

The Scott Arms serves tasty, wholesome, locally-sourced food throughout the year, either in the formal dining area, the two roomy bars or outside where the Jerk Shak serves up freshly barbecued Caribbean cuisine during the sunnier months. The team in this Dorset gem of a pub are very aware that a decent pint of locally-brewed real ale, well-respected cider, and a robust, eclectic wine selection keep its discerning customers happy.

Encombe Estate, home of William Culliford whose diligent detection during the late seventeenth century led to the suspension of thirty-eight Customs Officers.

## Piddletrenthide
**Piddle Inn**

Piddletrenthide, Dorchester DT2 7QF

Tel: 01300 348468

www.piddleinn.co.uk

Piddletrenthide lies in a valley of the Dorset Downs 8 miles north of Dorchester on the B3143 road and sits alongside the small River Piddle from which it takes its name. The villages of Piddlehinton and Puddletown lie to the south with Alton Pancras and Buckland Newton to the north. In the 2011 census the parish, which includes the small village of Plush to the northeast, had 323 dwellings and a population of 647.

The villagers of the Piddle Valley were early starters in the contraband trade, already thriving in these parts by about 1720, a time generally regarded as the dawn of the great smuggling age.

As early as 1718 it was reported that the village of Piddle, or Puddletown was: *'on the smugglers' highroad'*. In the following year two major incidents occurred at Piddletrenthide, known in those days as Collier's Piddle. The first occurred in November 1719, when sizeable quantities of smuggled goods were

As early as 1718, it was reported that the village of Piddle, or Puddletown was: *'on the smugglers' highroad'*.

This family-owned traditional inn takes its name from the chalk stream that flows through the beer garden. **Below:** In the days when local smugglers met here the pub was called The Green Dragon.

seized from Mr Harry Constantine, the village squire and William Dolling of the no longer extant Rose & Crown.

The contraband goods included bohea tea, coffee, cocoa beans, brandy, white pepper, muslin, canvas and French handkerchiefs – together worth then the considerable sum of £310. Constantine protested the goods had been lodged on his premises without permission but officials reported that: *'it is the opinion of most gentlemen in the country that he must know of it'* and orders were issued from Customs Officials for Constantine and his coachman, John Harding, to be prosecuted.

Within a month Customs Officials were back at Piddletrenthide searching for parcels of newly-landed goods, several of which were supposed to have been hidden in local houses. Now however, the villagers had received advanced warning of the raid and staged a mass evacuation. When Customs

The cosy front dining room is part of the original pub where smugglers gathered.

The Piddle Inn has been considerably extended at the rear providing space for the tastefully furnished, carpeted and decorated main bar/dining room.

The games area is a popular feature in this welcoming village local.
**Below:** At least two west-country ales are always available.

Men arrived they found the entire village deserted with every house locked up. Even the parish constable and the tithing-man were nowhere to be found.

This was a shrewd move by the local population, because without these parish officials, the Customs Men had no authority to enter or search any property. They waited several hours until darkness fell but still no-one appeared. Eventually, they were forced, in the words of Philip Taylor, the Weymouth Collector of Customs, to: *'return without doing anything, this being a case that frequently happens, and the smugglers take all advantage of the least misconduct of the officers.'*

Taylor's own superiors, the Commissioners of Customs in London, were not completely satisfied with this explanation and requested a further report from their Weymouth representative. This time Taylor wrote:

> *'It would have been inappropriate for all the officers of this town to guard the houses all night by reason of the danger of the mob, who appeared in great numbers and are always ready to insult us when they can do it undiscovered. It was most certainly the contrivance of the smugglers to send the parish officers from home, but they (and indeed the greatest part of the country) are all so firmly linked together in the smuggling trade that it will be impossible to prove collusion on them.'*

Piddletrenthide is a very long village which in Saxon times was divided into three tithings; each with its own mill. In 1787, William Oxford, of unknown age, worked one of the mills. His minor offence was probably concealing a small amount of contraband in the mill, for which he was fined £5, remitted to 50s or six months imprisonment.

In 1807, John Tibbs, a labourer in his twenties from Piddletrenthide was convicted of smuggling and fined £100 but bailed within twenty-four days, confirming a link with wealthy friends among the free trade fraternity or their customers. In 1822 a forty-six-year-old village carpenter, Henry Rogers, and Thomas Bagg, a twenty-three-year-old labourer were each convicted of smuggling and sentenced to a £100 fine or six months in Dorchester Gaol.

Dating from the 1760s this family-owned traditional inn takes its name from the chalk stream flowing gently through the beer garden; the perfect place to enjoy a relaxing summer meal and drink. The Piddle Inn offers an affordable range of quality homemade food and there are at least two well kept west country ales available.

Piddletrenthide is one of the Piddle valley's most attractive villages.

## Puncknowle
### Crown Inn
Church Street, Puncknowle DT2 9BN

Tel: 01308 897711

www.thecrowninndorset.co.uk

The Crown Inn was originally one of a terrace of seventeenth-century cottages housing families of agricultural labourers involved in the smuggling trade.

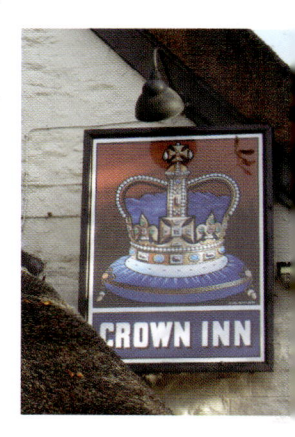

The quintessential West Dorset village of Puncknowle (pronounced Punnel) lies on the southern slopes of the Bride Valley approximately 5 miles east of Bridport and a-mile-and-a-half north of Chesil Beach.

West Dorset historian, George Roberts, writing within a few years of Isaac Gulliver's death said:

*'A smuggler named Gulliver kept forty or fifty men constantly employed who wore a kind of livery, powdered hair and smock frocks, from which they attained the name of 'White Wigs'. These men kept together and would not allow a few officers to take what they were carrying when the law was altered and seizures made from weaker parties. Gulliver amassed a large fortune and lived to a good age.'*

In addition to the large bar/dining room the comfortable beamed interior rambles through several areas opened up for dining. **Below:** New tenants, brothers Ed and Rob Watts have created an imaginative menu.

Gulliver was aged seventy-seven when he died in Wimborne in 1822, but was in his early thirties when he extended his operations into West Dorset. Contraband landed on the beach at West Bexington was conveyed by his 'White Wigs', directly north through Puncknowle at the start of its 65 mile journey to supply wealthy customers in the fashionable City of Bath.

Gulliver's standing army of up to fifty men would have included a number from Puncknowle itself whose names appear in Dorchester Gaol records for example; blacksmith James Chainey, aged twenty-eight who is described as having *'very large wide nostrils'*. Chainey was charged with smuggling in 1816 and sentenced to a £100 fine or sixteen months incarceration.

In 1822 two Puncknowle men both named William Churchill are listed. The couple were labourers and presumably father and son. William senior was sixty-four when found guilty of assaulting Customs Officers, remanded to Court at King's Bench and sentenced to a £100 fine or fourteen months. The younger William aged twenty-five was found guilty of unlawfully making a light on the sea coast. He was acquitted

Michael 'the Mayor of Puncknowle' whose mother was from the Northover smuggling family.

Visitors are encouraged to join in the fun with locals on quiz nights.

but found himself in trouble again the following year when he was given three months hard labour and £150 security to keep the peace for five years.

Also in 1822 John Tompkins, a twenty-eight-year-old fisherman, was accused of assaulting Customs Officers but acquitted and released after four weeks. In 1823, twenty-three-year-old labourer Thomas Hansford, was convicted of smuggling and given a fine £100 or one year in gaol. In 1834, twenty-one-year-old labourer Henry Seal was accused of smuggling and obstructing Customs Officers but was bailed and acquitted after six months.

*It would be hard to find a more enjoyable, welcoming atmosphere.*

At Swyre, adjacent to Puncknowle and a stone's throw from the beach, members of the Northover family were heavily involved with all aspects of free trading and frequent inhabitants of the smuggling wards in Dorchester Gaol. Michael, one of the present day regulars at the Crown Inn is descended from the Northovers on his mother's side and affectionately known as 'The Mayor of Puncknowle'. He took pains to explain to me how the family were forced into law breaking as a result of dire poverty.

The Crown Inn was originally one of a terrace of seventeenth-century cottages housing families of agricultural labourers

*For relaxed summer days and evenings there is a lovely garden overlooking the Bride Valley.*

involved in the smuggling trade. In the eighteenth century the original pub occupied the small cottage at the left hand end.

Friendly and welcoming to locals and visitors alike, the present day pub is popular with walkers, families and dog owners. In addition to the large bar/dining room the comfortable beamed interior rambles through several areas opened up for dining. Leather sofas and traditional fireplaces feature as part of the attractive mix.

For relaxing summer days and evenings there is a lovely garden overlooking the Bride Valley. Mature shrubs and extensive countryside views complete this peaceful oasis away from the hustle and bustle of everyday life.

New tenants, brothers Ed and Rob Watts, have created an imaginative cuisine and support their claim of using the best local produce by listing details of their suppliers on the menu. Starters include West Bay mussels, home-made smoked mackerel pâté and deep fried pheasant strips. Among the main courses on offer are West Bay fish pie, red onion and beetroot tart with cabbage mash and Dorset Longhorn rump steak in red wine sauce.

For those with room for dessert the selection includes iced pistachio and cherry nougat, wine poached pear and chocolate and spiced orange pave. Real ales are from Palmers, the local award-winning brewery.

This track leading from the beach at West Bexington was the start of the 65 mile journey to supply luxuries to wealthy customers in fashionable Bath.

Symondsbury presents the quintessential English village scene with a traditional thatched village pub close to the church.

## Symondsbury
### Ilchester Arms

Symondsbury, Bridport DT6 6HD

Tel: 01308 22600

www.theilchesterarms.com

'We believe the real pub is in danger but we must first attempt to define what we mean by a real pub. Providing a definition is not easy anymore than defining a great work of art is easy but, as with a great work of art, one knows when one is in the presence of the real thing.'

John Booth, *The Real Pub Guide*

Symondsbury Village is a hidden gem nestling beneath the local landmark of Colmer's Hill. Situated approximately 16 miles west of Dorchester and one and a half miles northwest of Bridport, bounded by the Marshwood Vale to the north and the World Heritage Jurassic Coast to the south.

With its source just north of Symondsbury parish the River Simene meanders through the village, meeting the River Brit to continue its journey to the sea at West Bay.

Symondsbury free traders were accustomed to waiting at the ready near the stretch of Chesil Beach around Seatown, Eype and West Bay on nights when the dark moon was passing in and out of cloud. Listening for a louder splash above the soft, rolling surf, they followed the sound of a muffled curse. Then, from the murky sea the dark shape of a boat emerged, being pulled up on to the shingle by shadowy figures.

Swiftly the village smugglers lent a hand unloading kegs and dragging them up the beach and on to the first stop hiding places in the village of Symondsbury and the surrounding countryside. Local cottages had obscure nooks and cavities

Brian and Gloria Dodge are the welcoming and experienced licensees of this characterful pub.

It's hard to resist the inviting built in high backed settle by the inglenook and the festooned fire surround resplendent with horse brasses and antique copper pans.

Well kept Palmers ales are served with a lovely smile.

The classically decorated dining room conveys a timeless charm.

in walls and roof spaces where tubs could be secreted. Farm outbuildings had large purpose built cellars with well camouflaged trap door entrances.

In 1730 Simon Roper of Symondsbury had his hay barn raided by Customs Officers who seized 3½ gallons of brandy from a cave below the threshing floor. This was not the first time Ropers had been in trouble with Preventive Men. In 1725 Richard Roper with his friend Joseph Trinkhole had 15 gallons of brandy and strong water (undiluted brandy) seized.

The same year Anthony Stephens of Symondsbury was apprehended riding a grey mare with two bottles of brandy in the sack bag slung over his saddle. Fifteen years later came evidence that smuggling still continued in Symondsbury

# SYMONDSBURY

*There is a gentle hum of conversation in the rustic bar when old friends meet.*

when thirty-four-year-old labourer Richard Prior was sent to Dorchester Gaol for six months.

The Ilchester Arms is a traditional thatched village pub full of character, an architectural historian's delight. The core of the building is fifteenth century with sixteenth-century oak beams salvaged from Tudor ships wrecked along the Jurassic Coast. Mullioned windows and a huge open fireplace in the bar further attest to the antiquity.

During the eighteenth and early nineteenth-century pub landlords often relegated all or part of the responsibility of running the pub to their wives whilst they pursued a secondary occupation. Former landlords of the Ilchester Arms have also been farmers, bakers, butchers and brewers with earlier generations of customers supplying them with smuggled brandy, rum and tobacco.

*The Ilchester Arms is family friendly and, as might be expected, dogs are also welcome.*

Dogs are welcome in the rustic open-plan bar which has a built-in high-backed settle by the inglenook, with the fire surround festooned with horse brasses and antique copper pans. There is a pretty restaurant with its own fire plus a skittle alley doubling as a family room. The brookside garden

The brookside garden in a natural setting is well stocked with tables and a separate children's safe play area.

in a natural setting is well stocked with tables and a separate safe children's play area.

Well-kept Palmers ales are served with a smile and there is a good range of enjoyable traditional food. The choices on the specials board include fresh fish dishes and vegetarian options. A reference on the menu *'Please take time to browse before choosing your meal'* sums up the ambience of this lovely pub.

Eype Beach below Thorncombe Beacon where contraband was landed and transported inland through Symondsbury village. (Picture by James Cook)

The Bridport Arms Hotel developed from a farmhouse built around the late seventeenth or early eighteenth century.

## West Bay, Bridport
### Bridport Arms Hotel

West Bay, Bridport DT6 4EN

Tel: 01308 422994

www.bridportarms.co.uk

West Bay is the harbour for the nearby market town of Bridport lying about a mile-and-a-half to the north. In 1832 the harbour opened a Customs House and achieved 'Bondport' status with the establishment of bonded warehouses, so becoming known as Bridport Harbour. However, with the coming of the Great Western Railway in 1884 it was promoted as a holiday resort and the name changed to help attract visitors.

Picnic tables stand in a forecourt area by the residential entrance.

The harbour's previous main commercial trade had been exporting rope and fishing nets for which Bridport was famous. Known today as 'The Golden Gateway to the Jurassic Coast', West Bay has a mixed economy of tourism and fishing with its two beaches, harbour and marina offering a perfect seaside location for family holidays.

With the pub in the background dockers convey unloaded goods to the Old Customs Warehouse.

Three hundred years ago things were very different. By 1719 smuggling along the Dorset coast had reached an unprecedented level and in October of that year a huge quantity of brandy and salt was brought ashore at West Bay and *'carried off by great numbers of the country people'* while Customs Officers looked on helplessly.

In 1728, Mordecai Sugg had *'2 gallons of brandy or strong waters seized from his house, The Full moon'*. Brandy in its undiluted state was known as 'strong waters' and the name of Mordecai's house suggests it was a drinking den. In 1735, John Rose the younger had 5¼ lbs of tea taken from his house and in 1741 William Penishin 48 lbs of tea seized from his warehouse.

One smuggler who knew West Bay and its harbour intimately was John (Jack) Rattenbury, born in Devon in 1778. He was a seaman and fisherman who turned to smuggling to earn a living for himself and family. On 17 April 1801 Rattenbury had married Dorset girl Anna Partridge from Lyme Regis and they set up home in the town. Many of Rattenbury's adventures took place along the coast from Lyme to Weymouth including Bridport Harbour.

After thirty years involvement in the free trade this *Rob Roy of the West*, was prevailed upon to relate his adventures and *Memoirs of a Smuggler* was published in 1837. From this we learn of an incident at West Bay when the accomplished seaman took charge of a vessel intending to pilot it out of the harbour. Unfortunately, the ship was boarded by the press gang before it could set sail and Rattenbury found himself on the quay facing the prospect of years away in the Navy. At that moment he noticed his wife approaching and asked the lieutenant commanding the press gang if he could speak to her. This was refused, so Rattenbury, a burly figure of a man, shook off the sailors restraining him and made a dash for freedom. In the resulting chase his wife grabbed the lieutenant, whereupon townspeople joined the scuffle allowing Rattenbury to make his escape.

After thirty years involvement in the free trade smuggler Jack Rattenbury became known as the '*Rob Roy of the West*'.

In his *Memoirs of a Smuggler* burly Jack Rattenbury tells of his escape from a press gang at West Bay harbour.

From West Bay the chief route for free trade traffic was north through Powerstock and Hooke, then over Toller Down where an inn called The Jolly Sailor, much frequented by smugglers had stood previously.

Court records show that Customs Officers did enjoy a limited success. In 1821, twenty-six-year-old shoemaker William Powell had a lucky break. He was caught smuggling and given the curiously calculated option of a £46.13s.2d fine or five and a half months in gaol. Good fortune attended him that day as he was discharged *'on account of His Majesty's coronation'*. Another shoemaker, thirty-one-year-old Sam Marsh was less fortunate in 1824 being sentenced to a £26 fine or 6 months incarceration, when thirty-seven-year-old labourer Seth Bishop was handed a similar punishment.

Although the pub otherwise has been greatly extended the flagstoned inglenook bar still retains a traditional feel.

In 1823 there is a record of thirty-six-year-old ropemaker and twine spinner Benjamin Powell caught smuggling and given a £50 fine or nine months imprisonment and fifty-year-old labourer William Gerrard £50 or five months. forty-two-year-old Richard Sheppwick with a seemingly good job as a sail-cloth weaver was gaoled for a month for smuggling.

An island server separates the simple bare-boards raised area at the front from the dining section of this spacious pub.

However, it is not just men's names appearing in the records of Lyme Regis Quarter Sessions. In the early 1820s the names appear of four Bridport women who were fined or imprisoned. They included two twine spinners, sixty-year-old blind widow Levia Rutledge and fifty-year-year-old Joan Stroud. Two shoe thread winders also were convicted, forty-five-year-old Ruth Hounsell and Susan Symes, one year her senior. thirty-six-year old Charlotte Drake of *'no trade'* was bailed in 1817 for assaulting and obstructing an Excise Officer. It was noted she was the wife of Henry Drake and *'lives at Bridport but belongs to Dartmouth, Devon'*.

The cosier carpeted dining area has more of a country kitchen feel with its wealth of sea and nostalgic prints.

Standing on the beach by the harbour at West Bay, this stylish thatched pub is the oldest surviving building hereabouts. Like many Dorset smugglers' pubs it is understood originally to have been a farmhouse from around the late seventeenth or early eighteenth century which operated initially as a cider house. On becoming a licensed pub it was named The Ship Inn but sometimes referred to as The Sloop, possibly because of its sign. Following a refurbishment in 1822 it re-opened as the Bridport Arms.

Beyond the original flagstoned inglenook bar, an island server separates the simple bare-boards raised area at the front of this spacious pub from the cosier carpeted dining section

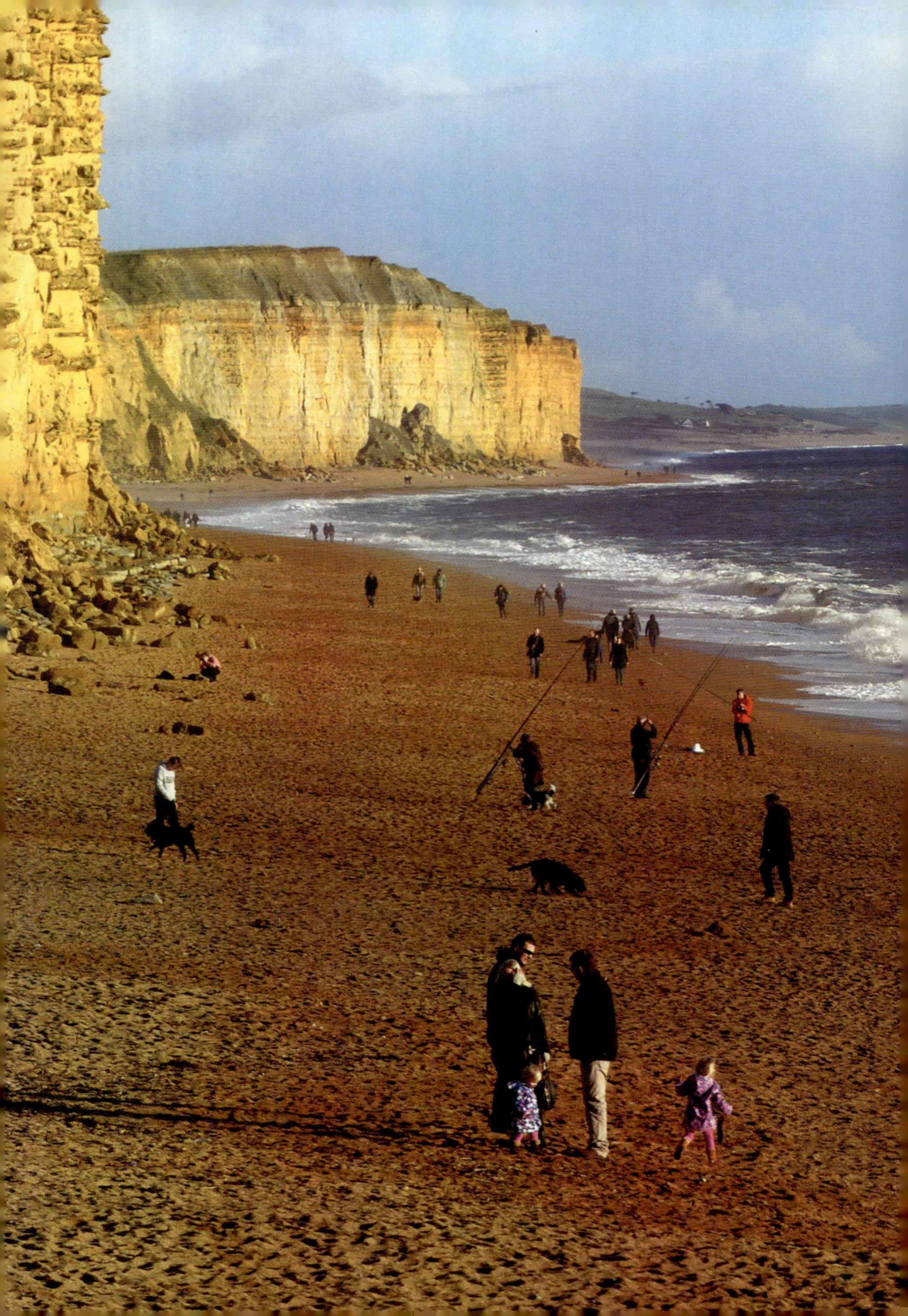

East Cliff dominates the contraband landing beach at West Bay which is popular today with fishermen and fossil hunters.

which displays a wealth of sea and nostalgic prints and has more of a country kitchen feel. Outside are picnic tables by the hotel's residential entrance.

The Bridport Arms is open to non-residents who are welcome to wine and dine in the pub bar and in the hotel restaurant well known for fish and seafood along with many other great locally sourced lunch and dinner dishes. Palmers ales are from the Old Brewery in Bridport, still standing on the original site where part of the building is thatched, and has been in continuous operation since 1794, the year after Jack Rattenbury embarked on his career as a privateer.

This stylish thatched hotel stands right on the beach by the harbour at West Bay.

# Wimborne
## The Olive Branch

6 East Borough, Wimborne BH21 1PF

Tel: 01202 884686

www.theolivebranchwimborne.co.uk

The enchanting market town of Wimborne Minster is rich in character and steeped in history; a town of ancient legends, kings and smugglers. Rising majestically above historic streets, riverside walks and pretty bridges is the twelfth-century Minster Church with its famous chained library. Interred in its tombs are King Ethelred of Wessex, Earl John Beaufort and the Duke and Duchess of Somerset. Perhaps surprisingly they all rest in company with Dorset's most legendary smuggler cum 'entrepreneur', Isaac Gulliver.

Gulliver was born in Wiltshire in 1745 at a time

*The Olive Branch, 6 East Borough, Wimborne, former home of Isaac Gulliver's granddaughter.*

when smuggling was in the ascendency and had already become a way of life for large sections of the community. In 1768, aged twenty-three, he married Elizabeth (Betty) Beale, a publican's daughter from The Blacksmith's Arms at Thorney Down, near Sixpenny Handley.

For a period, before moving nearer the coast, Isaac and Betty took over running the pub, and changed its name to The Kings Arms. During that time the surrounding area abounded with smugglers, poachers and rogues of every kind and once described as a man of 'herculean proportions', Isaac Gulliver was a natural leader with an innate flair for business. Wisely investing and spreading widely his ill-gotten gains he eventually employed a network of loyal contraband carriers. These porters and the bodyguards who protected them were recognisable by their white powdered wigs appearing more like gentlemen's servants than smugglers.

His eventual domain extended in every direction well beyond Dorset's borders. In partnership with Roger Ridout from Okeford Fitzpaine, Gulliver was reputed to be supplying the cities of Bristol and Salisbury along with markets as far afield as Warwick, Worcester and Oxford.

The wood panelling and moulded plaster ceilings in this cosy nook and in the larger dining room are original.

In later years, the socially ambitious Isaac and Betty lived in a succession of desirable houses in East Dorset, notably at Kinson, West Moors and Long Crichel. They had one son who died in his early twenties and two daughters who both married well. In 1793 their elder daughter, Elizabeth, wed William Fryer, a rich banker and businessman, receiving a dowry of local land holdings from her wealthy father.

In 1817, aged seventy-two, Isaac retired with his wife to a classically-proportioned Georgian house at 45 West Borough, Wimborne (acknowledged by a plaque to the left of the front door) where he lived for the remaining five years of his life.

By the time of his death at Wimborne in 1822 Gulliver had built a vast contraband empire, owned property spread over four counties and brokered a deal from the King for a pardon. He became a church warden at Wimborne Minster and is buried in the nave aisle between the two church wardens' seats. In this position his gravestone became excessively worn and was removed to be displayed on a wall in the church tower.

Ann Castleman (née Fryer), Isaac Gulliver's fortunate granddaughter.

**Below:** Respectable banker Edward Castleman.

Gulliver left bequests worth more than £20,000, some going to his daughter Elizabeth, considerably extending her original land holdings. These family investments, augmented by her husband's estate, included an interest in at least ten local pubs.

In 1823, a year after Gulliver's death, Elizabeth's daughter Anne (Gulliver's granddaughter) married Edward Castleman who, like his father-in-law, was a local banker. This fortunate union led to the amalgamation of the two banks, becoming known as the Fryer & Castleman Bank.

Initially the newlyweds took up residence in an attractive family owned house in East Borough (formerly Crooked

Borough), Wimborne now known as The Olive Branch. The Fryer & Castleman Bank later became Fryer Andrews & Company which in 1841 was incorporated with National Provincial Bank. Finally, in 1968, the bank merged with Westminster Bank and is now known as NatWest.

The Olive Branch at Wimborne differs from the other pubs featured in this book. It was not frequented by smugglers, indeed during the smuggling era was not a pub at all but a smart town house, which became a licensed premises only in 1967. It is included here because of the connection with Gulliver who made nonsense of the adage 'crime doesn't pay'.

The original Georgian house has been greatly extended at the rear to create a spectacular bar and restaurant. It was first licensed in 1967 and is currently owned by Blandford brewers, Hall and Woodhouse.

Patrons are always welcome to call in for a drink or coffee.

The 'Pantry', divided from the old part by the bar area, promotes a more relaxed dining style with long tables and benches.

The 'Herb Garden' with wicker chairs and tables and variety of plants leads to a more secluded riverside area.

In 1817, at the age of seventy-two, Isaac Gulliver retired to this desirable house at 45 West Borough, Wimborne, acknowledged by a plaque to the left of the front door.

The Stocks Inn at Furze Green a mile or two north of Wimborne, had extensive cellars and was used by Gulliver as a contraband clearing house.

The expansive interior comprises a variety of large spaces plus smaller nooks, crannies and annexes with a mix of wood and tiled floors and panelled walls. The formal beamed 'Dining Room' is built around an open kitchen providing opportunity for observing the culinary team at work. Another room known as 'The Pantry' affords a more relaxed dining style with long tables and benches. Customers may simply drop into the 'Bar' for a drink where the full range of Badger Beers is on offer. Adjacent to this the 'Beer Cave' annexe is a sight to behold with its curved ceiling made partly of beer bottles.

The Olive Branch is popular with families and groups due to its convenient town centre location, good value food and large gardens. The 'Herb Garden' with its wicker chairs and tables and variety of plants leads to a more secluded riverside area. Well-behaved dogs are welcome in the bar and gardens.

Isaac Gulliver became a church warden at Wimborne Minster and is buried in the nave aisle between the two church wardens' seats. **Inset:** Gulliver's gravestone became excessively worn and was removed to be displayed on a wall in the tower.

# Selected Bibliography

M. V. Angel  *In Search of Isaac Gulliver*

Roger Guttridge  *Dorset Smugglers*

Roger Guttridge and Carol Showell  *Smugglers' Trails (Pub Walks in Dorset)*

Thomas Hardy  *The Distracted Preacher* (from *Wessex Tales*)

Eileen Hathaway  *Smuggler (John Rattenbury 1778 – 1844)*

Beresford Leavens  *Isaac Gulliver, Le Contrebandier*

Geoffrey Morley  *Smuggling in Hampshire & Dorset*